SHAMANIC REGALIA

SHAMANIC REGALIA

IN THE FAR NORTH

PATRICIA RIEFF ANAWALT

109 illustrations

Thames & Hudson

For

The Reader: Alan Grinnell

The Recorder: Barbara Sloan

The Traveler: Kathleen Whitaker

Frontispiece: Tlingit shamanic masquette from southeast Alaska,
ca. 1840. Height 2¼" (5.7 cm).

Shamanic Regalia in the Far North © 2014 Patricia Rieff Anawalt

First published in 2014 in hardcover in the United States of America by
Thames & Hudson Inc., 500 Fifth Avenue, New York, New York 10110

thamesandhudsonusa.com

Library of Congress Catalog Card Number 2013950866

ISBN 978-0-500-51725-3

Printed and bound in China by Toppan Leefung Printing Limited.

CONTENTS

INTRODUCTION

The shaman's costume itself…discloses not only a sacred presence but also cosmic symbols and metapsychic itineraries. Properly studied, it reveals the system of shamanism as clearly as do shamanic myths and techniques.

—

Mircea Eliade[1]

＊

For anyone interested in the belief systems and traditions of ancient peoples, there are few items of apparel on this earth as informative as shamanic garments and accoutrements. Such ritual paraphernalia tends to retain and reflect the mindset of the ancient antecedents of cultures, which, if they still exist, may now be much-diluted. As a result, shamanic regalia offers a window into remote worldviews seldom available elsewhere. Some of the world's most intriguing shamanic attire existed among three major groups in the Far North: the land-based hunters and herders of Siberia; their nearby neighbors, the maritime sea hunters of the Arctic and Alaska; and the dramatic cultures of the Northwest Coast of present-day British Columbia. Given the generally accepted view that the Eskimos[2] of Alaska were the descendants of migrants from Siberia—and the expectation that the full range of shamanic traditions would have been inherited as well—it is puzzling to observe that these two groups had quite different shamanic regalia. The apparel used by Siberian shamans (1) was quite different than the ritual garb utilized in Alaska (2). Further, there is disagreement as to whether the Eskimo masking tradition influenced that of the Northwest Coast[3] (3) or if the initial influence moved in the opposite direction.[4] But before exploring these dissimilar styles in detail, it is first necessary to explain the terms "shaman" and "Far North."

1 (opposite) Siberian shamans usually wore body-encasing costumes, often heavily ornamented with iron attachments, but very seldom wore masks. Along the lower edge of this shaman's headdress is attached a vision-obstructing fringe, the so-called "blinker." The practitioner is using his ivory-and-wood baton to lash his "horse"—the drum—that he will ride into the realm of the spirits.

SHAMAN

The word "shaman" itself comes from the Tungas-speaking Evenk, hunters and reindeer herders of the northern taiga forests of central Siberia. Shamans served as curers, diviners, and prognosticators, but they were seldom "powerful" in their communities in a political sense. A shamanic destiny was often inherited, passed from father to son or, more frequently, from grandfather to grandson. While women also were sometimes called to become shamans, it was usually men who became practitioners. (Although a minority of practitioners were women, throughout this book "he" and "his" are used to refer to shamans in general, in order to avoid awkward repetition of "his or her," "he or she.")

This study focuses on paraphernalia revealed archaeologically or connected with shamans who were still practicing in small animistic societies in the Far North at the turn of the 19th/20th centuries. Rituals were performed to ensure success in healing, hunting, divination, and to augment a practitioner's ability to communicate between the earthly and spiritual realms. The shaman's cosmos was divided into three worlds, Lower, Middle, and Upper. In each realm, spirits were the main concern; with the aid of supernatural helpers, practitioners strove to manipulate their environment. The surviving objects connected with those ritual practices—examples of which illustrate this book—have bequeathed to us a unique sense of that animistic world, which reflects the early interactions between people and nature.

The academic response to shamanic studies has been a lively one, and particularly so following the publication of Mircea Eliade's 1964 English edition of *Shamanism: Archaic Techniques of Ecstasy*. One of his chief critics, Alice Kehoe,[5] points out that Eliade did not seem troubled that the data he used to define his shamanic "archaic substructure" came largely from ethnologic studies of modern practitioners.[6] Kehoe also contends that Eliade made no attempt to check the sources of his information, nor did he venture out into the field to actually investigate the practices of contemporary shamans. He truly was an "arm-chair" scholar in the tradition of Sir James S. Frazer, author of *The Golden Bough*, an

2 (opposite) Dramatic masks were the principal accoutrements of Alaskan shamans.

3 (opposite) An 1889 posed photograph of a mask-adorned Tlingit shaman treating an ill patient. The photograph is captioned, "Medicine Man Exorcising spirits from a Sick Boy."

encyclopedic compilation of travelers' tales and ancient legends first published in 1890. Nevertheless, Eliade has strongly influenced the field, and continues to do so.

Shamanism often has been referred to as the world's oldest religion. Many of these claims grow out of interpretations of the Upper Paleolithic cave art located in the southwest of France and beyond the Pyrenees in Spain. At such ancient sites as Chauvet (ca. 32,000 BC), Altamira (ca. 18,500 BC), and Lascaux (ca. 17,300 BC), viewers invariably describe their experience in memorable terms, as evidence Wade Davis:

> Reaching deep into the earth, through narrow passages that opened into chambers illuminated by the flicker of tallow lamps, men and women drew with stark realism the animals they revered, singly and in herds, using the contour of the stone to animate forms so dramatically that the entire caverns come alive even today with creatures long since lost to extinction.[7]

Over the past century, a number of respected archaeologists have published their interpretations of Paleolithic cave art. One of the more iconoclastic reviewers of those theories is the archaeologist Paul G. Bahn and his photographer Jean Vertut,[8] who note that invariably the explanations reflect the intellectual zeitgeist of their time:

- *Art for Art's Sake*: the theory that best suited the end of the 19th century;
- *Sympathetic/Hunting Magic*: a theory growing out of the ethnographic studies of the early 20th century;
- *Sexual and Structural Interpretations*: theories that arose during the 1950s and 1960s, the era of the sexual revolution, as well as through the influence of the structuralist Claude Lévi-Strauss;
- *Astrological/Astronomical Observations*: theories that developed during the Space Age;

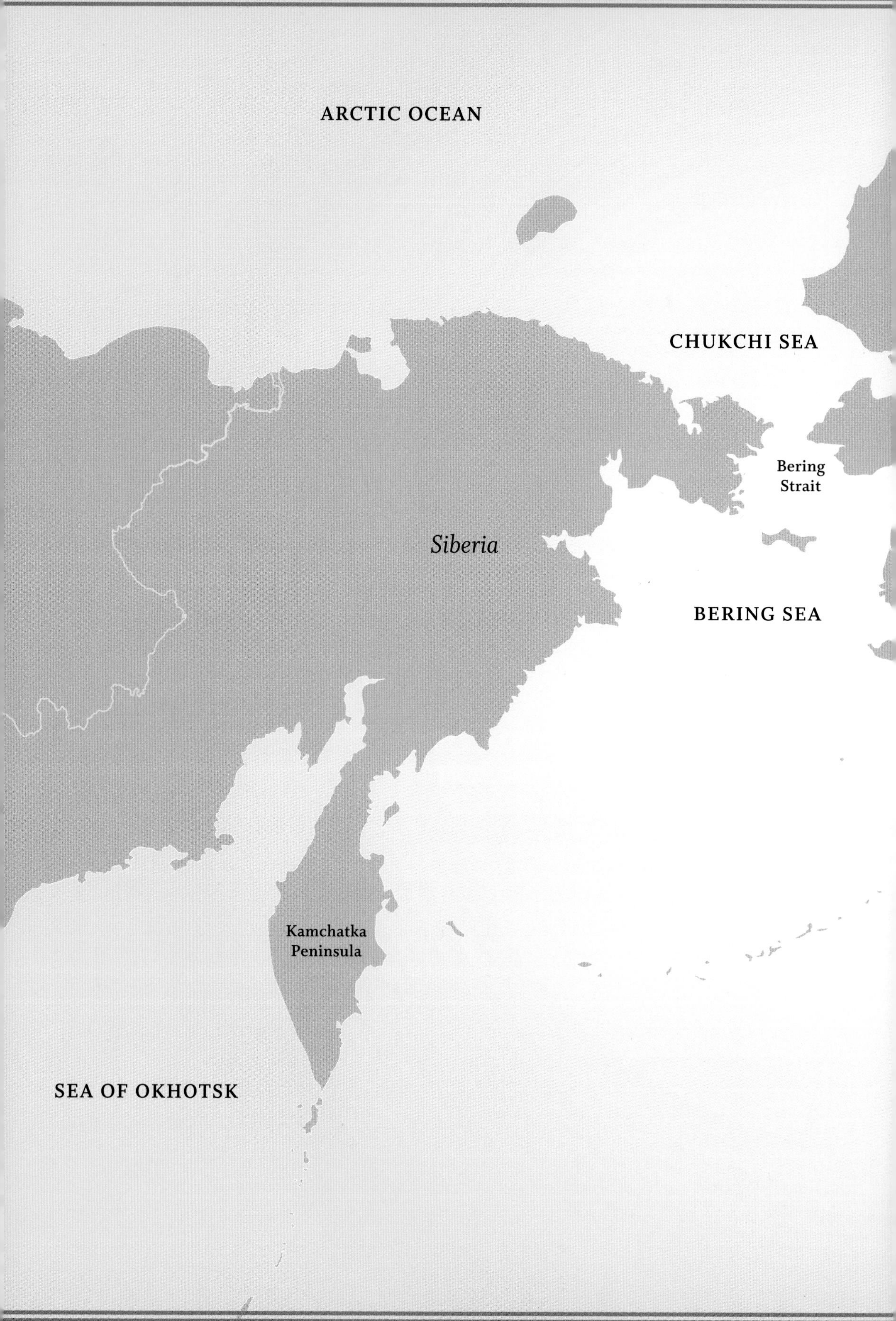

ARCTIC OCEAN

CHUKCHI SEA

Bering
Strait

Siberia

BERING SEA

Kamchatka
Peninsula

SEA OF OKHOTSK

Alaska

Bristol Bay

Aleutian Islands

GULF OF ALASKA

Northwest Coast

*British
Columbia*

PACIFIC OCEAN

N

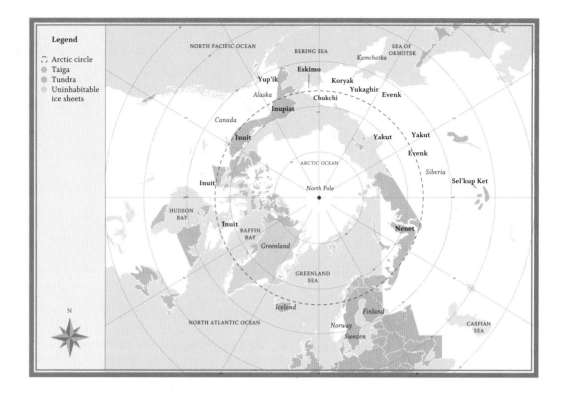

- *Shamanic Trance Explanations*: hypotheses reflecting New Age[9] interest in hallucinogenic phenomena and altered states of consciousness;
- *Information Theory*: a Computer-Age approach concentrating solely on the "quantity of information" inherent in each cave's painted figures without reference to an overall message.

It seems fair to assume that most of the cave art of the last Ice Age indeed did contain a "message" which was not aimed at us, and which we cannot understand clearly. Bahn challenges cave art explanations by asking, "…whether one is content to work with the art as a body of markings that cannot be read, or whether one wants to have stories made up about it."[10]

Whether or not shamanism—the art of influencing events through the aid of spirits—was mankind's earliest religion, it unquestionably is a very ancient practice that has survived as the world's most widespread belief system: there are thousands of small-scale ethnic groups around the globe who still have resident shamans.[11]

Map 1 (pages 14–15)
The Far North, including
northeast Siberia, the
Bering Strait, Alaska, and
the fjorded area of the
Northwest Coast of British
Columbia.

Map 2 (opposite) A bird's-
eye view of the Far North
(after Vitebsky 2001: 44).

THE FAR NORTH

The Far North is often associated with the term "Beringia," which refers to the Bering land bridge—now the Bering Strait—that joined present-day Alaska and eastern Siberia at various times during the Pleistocene Ice Age (Map 1). Because the Beringian region was never glaciated, much of Siberia and Alaska was accessible to human habitation; indeed, the area was part of a pan-North Pacific *oecumene*, an ensemble of related peoples integrated by trade, migration, warfare, and the cross-fertilization of ideas, oral traditions, and art into a large cultural universe.[12]

Northeast Siberia, Alaska, and British Columbia's Northwest Coast make up the rugged, remote lands that rim the North Pacific (Map 2). They were among the last regions on earth to be described by Western explorers and cartographers, despite the fact that the vast northern wilderness of mountains, forests, tundra, and ice geographically link the continents of Eurasia and North America. This study of shamanic regalia focuses on the arc of land and islands that surround the northern reaches of the Pacific Ocean and its component and adjacent seas (see Map 1): the Sea of Okhotsk, the Bering Sea, and—north of the Bering Strait—the Chukchi Sea.

> From Kamchatka to the Arctic Ocean, from the Aleutian Islands to the mountainous, fjorded coasts of British Columbia…[Western] explorers found the North Pacific rim inhabited by peoples well and warmly dressed and housed, equipped with ingenious and effective tools and weapons, organized in large groups with wide-ranging political and economic contacts, and possessed of complex religious beliefs, striking artistic traditions, often elaborate social institutions, and a vast practical knowledge of the environment.[13]

These resourceful northern people also maintained a long-established, ongoing tradition of shamanism.

I

SIBERIA

It was of crucial importance that shamanic power be reflected in dress and regalia…Piers Vitebsky reports that the first question one hears when there is a rumor of a new Siberian shaman is, "Yes, but has he got the costume?" For a shaman, looks count.

✳

Some 5,000 to 10,000 years ago various tribes of Tungus-speaking nomadic hunters moved across the temperate regions of eastern Asia into the virgin forests of northeastern Siberia, and then further north and east until some of the migrants crossed into the Americas via the Beringia land bridge (see Map 1).[1] It is generally accepted that in those early times, the worldview of all of the nomadic hunters was that of supplicants dependent on appeasing the spirits of their prey so the animals would cooperate in the hunt and thus enable the vulnerable humans to survive in the Far North's extremely harsh environment (5). In Asia, however, that cosmology of collaborative reciprocity began to change some 2,000 years ago when the Siberians made two important advances: first, they domesticated reindeer, and, second, they obtained metallurgy. Interestingly, neither of those innovations ever took hold in pre-contact Alaska.

The cultures of northeastern Siberia with which this study is involved (Map 3) include: the Yukaghir people of far eastern Siberia, living in the basin of the Kolyma River; the Chukchi, a reindeer-herding group located adjacent to the Chukchi Sea; and the Koryak of the northeast Kamchatka Peninsula and adjacent maritime regions. The Koryak were divided between reindeer breeders in the interior and sea mammal hunters on the coast. These groups are to be distinguished from the central Siberian Sel'kup, the Evenk (Tungus), and the Yakut, who bordered the northeastern Siberian Paleoasiatics on the west and from whom they acquired many features of their technology, clothing, and art, as well as their reindeer economy.[2] Among all of these

4 (opposite) A young Koryak shaman reviving from the exertion of a healing séance.

5 (below) The great wilderness of mountains, forests, tundra and ice that make up the Siberian Far North.

groups, shamanism was still actively practiced at the turn of the 19th and 20th centuries.

Siberian reindeer domestication and breeding began somewhere to the southwest of Lake Baikal among the Tungus-speaking ancestors of the modern-day Evenk.[3] This breakthrough, which probably took place around the beginning of the first millennium AD, may have developed as a result of contact with the horse-breeding cultures of the Turks and Mongols of Central Asia. Although horses do not thrive on the tundra, the ancient Tungus began to experiment with using horse saddles on their indigenous reindeer, which they already had partially tamed but were then using only as lures for hunting wild reindeer.

The saddling experiment proved successful and the concept of reindeer as human transport was born (6). Further, the Evenk began selectively breeding their reindeer in order to create larger and stronger animals than those in neighboring herds: in trade, one Evenk reindeer became worth two from nearby groups.

6 (above) Reindeer used as human transportation: a bride riding to her wedding.

Map 3 (pages 24–25) Northeast Siberia with the illustrated shamanic costumes (see 1, 8, 13, 15, 22, 25, 27, 30, 32) shown in their places of origin.

POWER AND RITUAL

One of the core beliefs of worldwide shamanism is that the soul of a shaman in trance had the power to leave the body and travel to other parts of the cosmos, soaring high into the heavens or plunging deep into the earth. Siberian shamans were commonly drawn or painted as skeletons (7), representing their physical dismemberment by spirits during a traumatic initiation when they were tortured and dismantled before subsequently being reconstructed.

ARCTIC OCEAN

Nenet

Tobol Province

Turukhan Territory

**Evenk
(Tungus)**

Sel'kup

Yenisei Province

Tomsk Province

Irkutsk Province

*Semipalatinsk
Region*

Uriankhai Territory

*Semirechensk
Region*

CHUKCHI SEA

Chukchi

Yukaghir

Yakut Region

Yakut

Koryak

Maritime Region

SEA OF OKHOTSK

**Evenk
(Manegry)**

Maritime Region

*Sakhalin
Region*

*Transbaikal
Region*

Amur Region

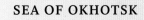

N

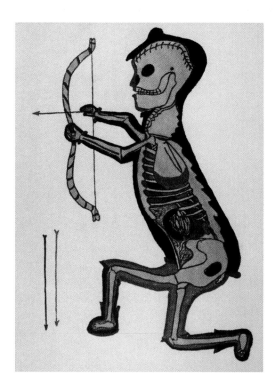

7 (left) Siberian shamans were often drawn as skeletons in reference to their traumatic initiations by spirits, who tortured and dismantled a neophyte before reassembling his or her body.

8 (opposite) A Yukaghir shaman's coat embellished with iron "ribs" in reference to the practitioner's traumatic initiation by the spirits.

Many Siberian costumes commemorate that skeletal phase of a practitioner's evolution through the addition of distinctive pieces of iron and copper to a ritual coat, often representing ribs (8). Throughout much of the area there has long been a special relationship between shamans and blacksmiths, those skilled craftsmen who made the practitioners' dramatic, metal-adorned attire possible.[4] It must be noted, however, that not all Siberian shamanic costumes were adorned with metal (see 13, 15).

In Siberian rituals, it was of crucial importance that shamanic power be reflected in the dress and regalia of a practitioner. The shamanic authority Piers Vitebsky reports that the first question one hears when there is a rumor of a new Siberian shaman is, "Yes, but has he got the costume?"[5] For a shaman, looks count. According to most authorities, a practitioner's charm-laden coat was sometimes considered vital to the whole shamanic drama. Some of the

metal pieces found on a shaman's costume referred to animals who served as his helping spirits; others attested to the attained rank of the distinguished shaman himself. As can be imagined, the whole shamanic assemblage jangled fiercely—the noise was said to attract friendly spirits—and could weigh up to 50 pounds (almost 23 kg) (see 1). Indeed, one of the marks of a true shaman was the ability to handle the heavy, ungainly attire easily.

ON BECOMING A SIBERIAN SHAMAN

The shamanic gift was sometimes inherited, often skipping a generation, but not just anyone could become a shaman. The spirits would enter the person they chose, and force him (more rarely her) to become their servant. Certain physical traits were considered to be evidence of the spirits calling the future practitioner to the profession, and served to identify a shaman to his family. "Among most Siberian peoples, it was believed that the spirits would 'choose' a future shaman while he was in a special psychic state—the so-called 'shaman illness'—when the chosen one would seem to have lost his reason."[6] Usually this affliction occurred between the ages of five to fifteen; less often, between forty and fifty.

Becoming a professional shaman was a long process. Among the Evenk, it took between seven and twelve years just to qualify as a neophyte; "during this time, the novice would learn the practices and perfect the skills under the tutelage of an experienced shaman."[7] All of this preparation led to a shamanic position that carried with it many obligations and requirements, including the need to constantly improve the skills of memory, creative imagination, intuition, and organizational abilities.

Young shamans had to go through a series of initiation rites; with the Evenk it consisted of three stages. An initiation ritual could last a number of days with an old shaman conducting the ceremony, utilizing all of his regalia. The new practitioner would first receive his apron (9) together with a wood-and-ivory baton (10), a

9 (opposite) A Yukaghir shaman's apron, which closely resembles the Yukaghir women's similar garment. The Russian literature refers to shamanic aprons as "breast plates."

10 (left) A shaman's wood-and-ivory baton, which acted as a mediator between the spirit and human worlds. It also served as a lash to drive the shaman's mount (the drum; see 1). Length 13" (33 cm).

11 (right) A shaman's staff, which was used for a novice's first séance. Length 30" (77 cm).

12 (opposite) The back of a shaman's drum, elaborated to honor the loon, a pathfinder for a shaman because the bird—like the practitioner—could function under the water, on its surface, and in the air. Height 29½" (75 cm).

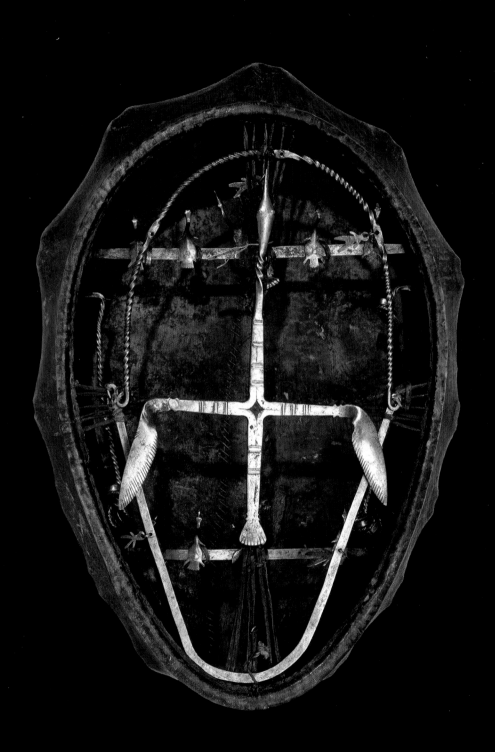

staff (11)—used for the novice's first séance—and a drum (12). The baton, one of the first accessories received by a young shaman, acted as his mediator between the spirit and human worlds; it also served as a lash to drive the shaman's mount—his drum—which he "rode" into the realm of the spirits (see 1).[8] Once the novice had received these first-stage professional attributes,[9] he then had to demonstrate his ability to use them, as well as to prove the limits of his own endurance, which had to be sufficient to sustain the demanding procedures involved in long and complicated rites.

The final stage of becoming a shaman occurred only after an acolyte had received his own guardian spirit, which usually appeared in the form of an animal or bird. The most common of these guardians were the wolf, the bear, the raven, the seagull, and the eagle.[10] But, of course, the new practitioner also needed recognition of his new status from those around him. Even after attaining a standing in the community as a fully initiated shaman, however, most professionals also had to maintain a day-to-day job in order to support themselves.

SIBERIAN REGALIA

Most of the shamanic regalia featured in this study was collected over the past 100-plus years, often under extremely difficult conditions. This was true throughout the Far North; Siberia is a case in point. At the turn of the 19th and 20th centuries, Siberia was a truly remote land, one infamous for its severe climatic conditions. Further, the indigenous peoples harbored firmly held, archaic religious concepts and treasured the sacred objects connected with their beliefs, items which they seldom wished to sell.

> Local inhabitants would trace the causes of illness—and even the death
> of loved ones or misfortune in a family that assisted museum staff in their
> [collecting] work—to the sale of cult objects. It was quite risky to purchase
> shaman's drums and garments, and particularly dangerous to take cult
> objects from sacred places and burial sites.[11]

Most of the collected Siberian pieces now reside in the great museums of the United States, Canada, Europe, and, especially, in Russia. The collection of the Russian Museum of Ethnography relating to shamanism of the peoples of Siberia and Russia's Far East is currently the largest in the world.[12] In the early 20th century, one of the first fieldworkers to make a significant contribution to the building of those collections was the well-known local historian, tax collector, and member of the Russian Geographic Society, P. E. Ostrovskikh. The two drums and batons that he acquired from the Sel'kup were the first such objects to enter the Museum's collection of important shamanic regalia.

In 1904, on an expedition to the Altai region, the director of the Ethnographic Department of the Russian Museum, D. A. Klementz, was also able to acquire some particularly interesting drums. While subsequently overseeing the new Museum's collection activities, Klementz actively involved correspondents of the Museum in amassing further collections. Among those was A. V. Adrianov, as well as the political exile Felix Yakovlevich Kon.[13] Sadly, space does not permit a full listing of the remarkable men of the early years of acquisition who worked so diligently, under truly difficult conditions, to collect Siberian shamanic material, objects that otherwise would have been lost to us forever.

Gratitude is also owed to the American Museum of Natural History for sponsoring the collection of much northern material under the auspices of the Jesup North Pacific Expedition, 1897–1902, a major foray into northeast Siberia, Alaska, and the Northwest Coast of British Columbia. That expedition, whose purpose was to investigate the relationship between people on either side of the Bering Strait—separated by only 55 miles (88 km) of open sea—was sponsored by the president of the Museum, the industrialist-philanthropist Morris Jesup; Franz Boas, subsequently founder of American Anthropology, served as the Expedition's Scientific Director.

The members of the Jesup Expedition included several significant figures in American and Russian anthropology and produced a number of important ethnographies as well as valuable collections of photographs and artifacts.

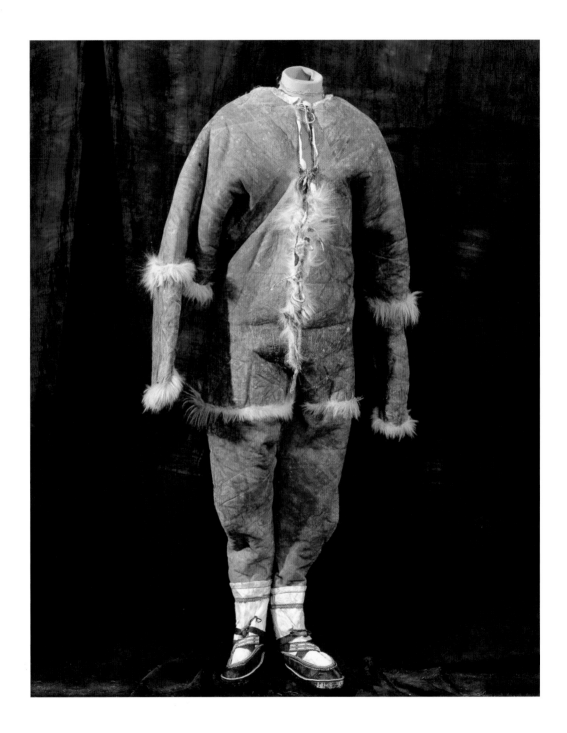

Among these objects are Siberian shamanic items collected by two outstanding Russian scientists. Vladimir Bogoras (1865–1936) and Vladimir Jochelson (1855–1937) were intellectual friends and colleagues who, in their youth, had been exiled for revolutionary activities to Siberia, where they became ethnologists. These remarkable men—and their equally outstanding, and beautiful, wives—made many valuable contributions to our understanding of northeastern Siberia. Most of the Jesup-collected material now resides in the American Museum of Natural History in New York.

THE RIGORS OF SIBERIAN FIELDWORK

The Siberian operation of the Jesup North Pacific Expedition covered an immense area; three sets of investigators were needed to carry out the fieldwork. The two northern teams were headed by the Russians Bogoras and Jochelson. Bogoras traveled extensively in the Chukota area among the Chukchi and Siberian Yup'ik people while his wife, Sofya Bogoras—who acted as photographer—made collections in the vicinity of Anadyr. Working conditions were terrible; famine and disease were rampant, and Bogoras almost died of influenza. Nonetheless, together these intrepid fieldworkers collected 5,000 artifacts in just eighteen months, together with folk tales, texts, skull and anatomical measurements, many wax cylinder recordings, and a woman's costume of a cross-dressing Chukchi shaman (13).

Vladimir Jochelson, together with his wife, Dina Brodsky Jochelson—who served as photographer, physician, and physical anthropologist—were assigned to study the Koryak and Yukaghir,[14] herders all. The couple arrived in the reindeer-herding Koryak area only to find that, due to a devastating measles epidemic the preceding winter, the group they sought had moved. Undaunted, the Jochelsons set forth to follow the Koryak, who had climbed far up into the mountains to

13 (opposite) The woman's costume of a cross-dressing male Chukchi shaman. Cross-dressing practitioners were considered the most powerful among the Chukchi, who held that "woman is a natural shaman."

14 (overleaf) Dina Brodsky Jochelson emerging from an underground house during the Jochelsons' fieldwork among the Koryak.

15 (opposite) A Tungus-speaking Evenk shaman dressed in full regalia; the six garments that make up his complete costume appear in illustrations 16–19.

escape the epidemic. The Russians' subsequent fieldwork was consistently trying; the couple frequently were living in underground houses (14), sometimes together with entire families, whose squalid conditions, lack of room, odor of blubber, and ever-present lice must have been truly oppressive. It was while staying among these people that the Jochelsons observed ceremonies that provide valuable insight into Siberian shamans' séance methods.

Jochelson[15] tells of a young Koryak shaman who, despite being described as "a bashful youth," nonetheless agreed to demonstrate his skill. Accordingly, the oil-lamps in the underground house were extinguished and the shaman began to beat his drum and sing. His voice, growing ever stronger, began to come from different areas of the dwelling in a most impressive manner: the youth was a skilled ventriloquist. In addition, the beat of the drum also began to resound from various parts of the area as the shaman moved noiselessly about, but always observed by the ever-alert Jochelson. Suddenly the drum and the singing stopped altogether. When the lamps were relit the exhausted shaman was found stretched out on a white reindeer skin declaring dramatically that "disease" had now left the village (see 4).

Jochelson relates another shamanic experience also involving a Koryak practitioner who, in the midst of his performance, suddenly asked the scientist for his knife: the spirits had told the shaman he must cut himself with the Russian's dangerously sharp traveling knife, which—despite Dina Brodsky Jochelson's concern—her husband reluctantly handed over. The shaman resumed beating his drum and sang to the spirits that he now was ready to carry out their demand. Suddenly, putting his drum aside, the shaman emitted a rattling sound from his throat and thrust the knife into his breast up to the hilt. Jochelson, ever the sharp-eyed observer, noted that after the shaman had cut through his jacket he immediately turned the knife downward. The shaman then drew out the knife, while again uttering the rattling sound in his throat, and resumed beating his drum.

Contrary to Jochelson's expectations, the shaman returned his knife and, through the hole in the jacket, displayed spots of blood on his body which, the Russian points out, must have been placed there previously.

Jochelson's response to this shamanic display is worth noting. The scientist cautions that the performance cannot be looked upon as a mere deception:

> Things visible and imaginary are confounded…the shaman himself may
> have thought that there was, invisible to others, a real gash on his body, as
> had been demanded by the spirits. The common Koryak are sure that the
> shaman actually cuts himself and that the wound heals up immediately.[16]

SIBERIAN SHAMANIC COSTUMES

In the collection of the American Museum of Natural History is a complete shaman's costume (15–21) acquired by Jochelson from a Tungus-speaking Evenk shaman on the shores of the Sea of Okhotsk. This practitioner—who obviously had traveled far—mentioned having come into contact with the Koryak, but their shamanic attire is decidedly different, as is discussed below.

Jochelson first describes the shaman's apron—the Russian literature refers to such garments as "breast plates"—which is made out of reindeer hide (17; also see 9 for a comparable Yukaghir apron). On the chest are figures of men cut out of cloth, which are called "dolls," literally "representations of human figures," who are the helpers of the shaman. Except for these sewn-on figures, the shaman's apron has the same appliqué decorations, embroideries, fringes, and tassels as Evenk women's aprons. Sexual ambiguity and transvestism were common features of Siberian shamans. Male practitioners often adopted female names, behaved like women and wore women's clothing (see 13).

The back of the shaman's coat (18) is described by Jochelson as being decorated with "conventionalized" figures (stylized drawings?) of human beings, embroidered in sinew thread,

16 (opposite) The Evenk shaman's cap, adorned with iron horns representing those of a wild reindeer, the spirit protector of the shaman.

17 (pages 42–43) The Evenk shaman's apron, made of reindeer hide and decorated with cloth cut-outs of human figures, the shaman's helpers. His apron closely resembles those worn by Evenk women.

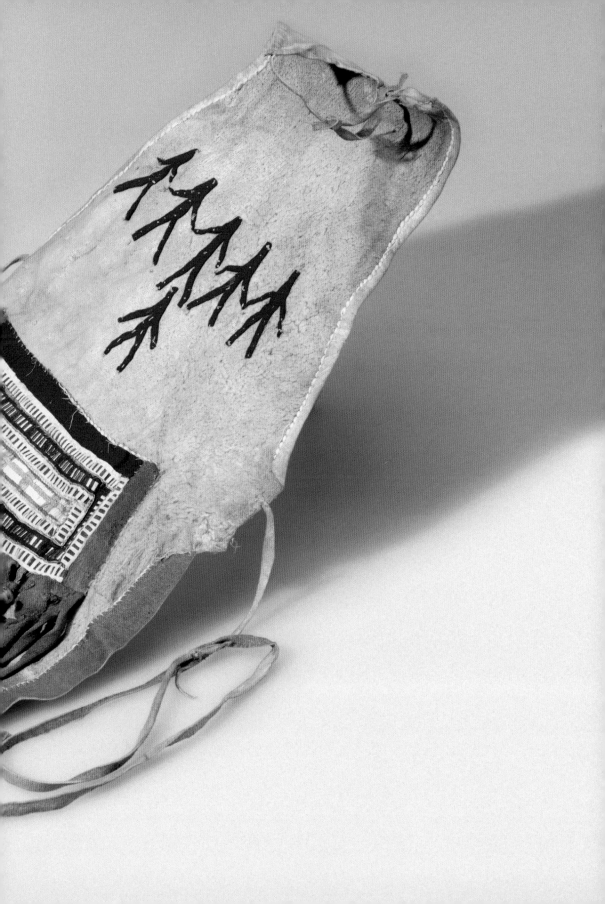

18 Back view of the Evenk
shaman's coat, decorated with
stylized drawings and tassels.

19 The front of the Evenk shaman's coat, decorated only with its orange-and-black borders and a few strings.

20 (pages 46–47) The Evenk shaman's gloves, decorated with embroidered designs in the "joint motif pattern." Fur emerges from the fingers of the left-hand glove, indicating that the shaman is in the process of transforming into a bear.

21 (above) The Evenk shaman's leggings, made of single pieces of soft reindeer leather; the foot sections have been reinforced with sturdy moose hide.

representing shamanic spirits. The tassels on the coat's back are called "poles," referring to the structure of the lower, cylindrical foundation of a Tungus tent. On the front borders of the coat (19) there are no decorations, figures or pendants, except for the garment's colorful border and a few leather strings.

The shaman's cap (16) is adorned with iron horns representing those of a wild reindeer, the spirit protector of the shaman. On the body of the cap conventionalized figures of men and animals are depicted, using sinew thread. Among the animals are the wolf and the snake, representing a class of shamanic helpers that differ in power from the wild reindeer spirit. The shaman's leggings (21) are made of single pieces of soft reindeer leather; the foot sections have been reinforced with sturdy moose hide.

The most intriguing items of the shaman's apparel are his gloves (20). Both are decorated with similar embroidered designs in the "joint motif pattern." The most arresting aspect, however, is the fur that emerges from the fingers of the left-hand glove, indicating that the shaman is in the process of transforming into a bear.

As a critically important aspect of a shaman's practice, the costume of most Siberian practitioners incorporated aspects of the cosmos as well as of the shaman's helper spirits in the form of animals and birds. Three further shamanic costumes are examined below, each collected in a different section of Siberia, each reflecting a different ethnic group. The first (22–24) is a late 19th-century Yakut shaman's coat collected in 1907 in the Yakut region of eastern Siberia (see Map 3). The three views of the coat are from the front, side, and back. The garment itself is made of reindeer skin adorned with important metal objects:

> Many details of the costume symbolizing bird feathers are reminiscent of a shaman's helper spirit. Along the hem hang long plaits strung with beads and copper tubes symbolizing snakes. The metal pieces represent the bones of a human

22 (overleaf, left) Back view of a Yakut shaman's iron-encrusted coat. Below the lancet-like pendants—a reference to birds' feathers—hangs a strap, which allows the shaman's assistant to hold onto the practitioner so the spirits cannot carry him away.

23 (overleaf, right) Side view of a Yakut shaman's iron-encrusted coat, showing the metal ribs and arm bones.

skeleton. Thus the shaman's costume, which represents his guardian spirit and is a shield against evil spirits, resembles both a human and a bird. On the back are straps that have both a functional and a symbolic significance. They would be used to hold on to the shaman during the séance and thus were considered the shaman's "reins." The Yakut shamans called themselves "people of the solar *ulus* with reins behind their backs."[17]

The second costume (25–26) is that of an important Sel'kup shaman; it consists of an outer coat, an apron, a headdress, and elaborate footwear. Only "great" or powerful shamans had such magnificent apparel. The coat is made of roughly cured wild, male reindeer skin; the back of the coat (26) has attached to it an array of helper spirits: frogs, a taimen—a Siberian salmon— and, at the shoulder level, pairs of double-headed loons. In Siberia, it was believed that the loon assisted as a shaman's pathfinder in all three of the cosmic realms of the shamanic universe: the bird is capable of functioning underwater, on the water's surface, and high up into the air.

Along the bottom of the shaman's coat two rows of metal images are attached: the shaman's helper spirits. The first row are metal anthropomorphic figures that comprise the shaman's army. The second row are frogs. It was believed that, during the Great Flood, a frog had saved humans by plugging a hole in the boat with its body. There are tubular adornments on the sleeves and across the back of the shaman's coat. "Fringe representing bird feathers is sewn to the sleeves, and there are four flat iron pieces attached to the sides of the parka representing ribs and at the same time serving as the shaman's 'shield'."[18] When in confrontation with evil spirits, a practitioner's clothing served as his armor.

Beneath the shaman's outer coat (25), he wears an apron of reindeer suede—leather finished with a napped texture— that is bordered with bear fur and decorated with metal

24 (opposite) The front of the Yakut shaman's coat depicts his spirit assistants.

25 (overleaf, left) The costume of an important Sel'kup shaman includes coat, apron, headdress, and elaborate footwear.

26 (overleaf, right) The back of the Sel'kup shaman's coat, showing metal pendants, ribs and a row of anthropomorphic figures, the shaman's army. At the hemline is a row of frogs, the shaman's helpers.

ornaments so as to protect the shaman's chest. His footwear is made of wild reindeer hide, fur side inward. Fixed to the calf is an "iron calf bone" and red cloth fringe under the kneecap represents blood vessels. "A bear's paw…is attached over the [toes]. The bear was considered a 'strong' spirit that protected the shaman and was connected with the Lower World."[19] Thus the bear could protect the shaman when he descended to the depths.

The shaman's metal headdress was a particularly prestigious aspect of his apparel; it was shaped in the form of a crown

> …to which was attached an arc topped with a representation of reindeer antlers. The shaman would receive it only after seven years of shamanistic practice. By putting it on he would "turn into" the celestial reindeer. The red cloth ribbons with bells and beads attached to the rim and falling below the knees symbolized plaits spirits could climb to the shaman from below as [he passed] along a path. The [accoutrements attached to such a] shaman's costume reflects the conception of the shaman as a bird-animal.[20]

A shaman's costume had to be symbolically "brought to life," and such rituals took place in springtime, "when the migratory birds returned."[21] A "reviving ritual" would be carried out by old and experienced shamans. This ceremony consisted of a procedure in which a practitioner would reconstruct reindeers from their skins, which subsequently would be used to create shamanic drums and garments. To activate the metal pendants, the shaman would call on a blacksmith to infuse the full magic power into each piece that he had created.[22]

The third shamanic costume to be considered is from the Koryak area, located in the Okhotsk Kamchatka region (see Map 3). Jochelson is somewhat uncertain about this "shaman's jacket;" he states:

> …one embroidered jacket [27] and headband [28] were sold to me for my collection as the garb used by the Altor shamans; but the jacket looks like

27 A Koryak male shaman's reindeer-skin coat.

28 (overleaf) A Koryak shaman's headband.

29 (pages 60–61) A Koryak female shaman wearing a simple costume reminiscent of 27, as she conducts a séance.

30 The elaborate costume of a female shaman from the Evenk Manegry area. The three vents on the front of her coat represent the entrances to the three worlds of the universe. Also note the vision-obstructing fringe in front of her face, the "blinker."

31 Back view of the female
shaman's costume.

32 A Guardian Spirit of Traditional Pursuits from the
Nenet people of western Siberia. This sacred object
is composed of seven cloth robes, one atop the other,
plus a belt. The cast-iron mask emerging from the
pocket dates from the Iron Age, ca. 1200 BC.

an ordinary dancing-jacket used in the whale festival, except that it has some small tassels which have apparently been borrowed from a Tungus shaman.[23]

Despite Jochelson's ambivalence regarding this male attire, in the same chapter he includes a photo of a female Koryak shaman (29) wearing a garment somewhat similar to the jacket he bought (27), as she beats her drum and conducts her ceremony.

Although Koryak female shamans wore simple attire, that certainly was not the case in other sections of Siberia, as illustrations 30 and 31 make clear. This costume, collected in 1910, was worn by an Evenk Manegry woman living in eastern Siberia, the Amur region (see Map 3). The three vents in the front of her caftan symbolize the entrance to the three worlds of the universe; the jingles and small bronze disks symbolize her "armor." The headdress of this costume is in the form of an iron crown, to which are attached symbolic reindeer antlers, jingles, and vari-colored cloth strips. It has been said that the jingles symbolize the shaman's dog helper spirits.[24] Notice, too, the vision-obstructing fringe in front of her face, the so-called "blinker."

AMULETS, MASKS AND SPIRITS

In addition to complete shamanic costumes, a brief reference must be made to Siberian guardian spirits and amulets. The Siberian Nenets believed that anyone fortunate enough to view the Guardian Spirit of Traditional Pursuits (32) would be blessed with good luck.[25] This sacred object consists of seven cloth robes layered one atop the other and then belted; an iron bow is tied to the belt. There is a cast-bronze anthropomorphic mask in the pocket of the top robe. Apparently, such masks, dating from the Iron Age, ca. 1200 BC, still can be found in the ground throughout western Siberia.[26]

Among ritual images of guardian spirits of the Evenk of eastern Siberia, masks were held in a special reverence as they were considered the soul or spirit of a shaman's ancestors (33). However, practitioners rarely wore such masks during séances, but instead placed them in an honored location within

33 (opposite) A string of masks that served as guardian spirits for the Evenk of eastern Siberia. Shamans rarely wore such masks during séances, but rather hung them in an honored location within their dwellings. Height of masks 6–9" (15–23 cm).

34 (below) The Koryak of eastern Siberia carved anthropomorphic figures out of tree branches to serve as guardian spirits. Height 13¾" (35 cm).

their dwellings. For the Koryak of eastern Siberia, anthropomorphic figures carved from an appropriately branched tree (34) could serve as symbolic guardian spirits. "During rituals the reindeer herders would 'feed' these images with the marrow and blood of sacrificial reindeer. Koryaks living on the coast would feed them with the fat and blood of the sea mammals they hunted."[27]

Apropos of amulets, wooden images were also used in healing. This anthropomorphic carving (35), sans arms or legs, is a hunchback with scars on its face; it was created in order to treat a form of bad back. During the shamanist healing séance, the figure would be hung on the belt of the patient and the shaman would proceed to "transfer" the illness to the amulet. Such shamanic aids have ancient roots, as evidence the "Nefertiti" of the Amur (36),[28] a

35 (opposite) Simple wooden pieces also served as amulets in healing. This 19th-century Namai (Goldy) figure, sans arms and legs, is a hunchback; its purpose is to treat a bad back. During a séance, the figure would be hung on the belt of the patient and the shaman would "transfer" the illness to the amulet. Height 9¼" (23.5 cm).

36 (right) "Nefertiti" of the Amur, a cast of an ancient clay female bust dating from the Siberian Neolithic, 4th–3rd millennia BC, which was used as a shaman's healing aid. Height 3¾" (9.5 cm).

burnished, fired clay female bust dating to the 4th to 3rd millennia BC, the Siberian Neolithic. Such figures are known as *sevoms*, spirits of illness and shaman's helpers.[29]

⁕

In this review of shamanic practices and regalia, it is important to emphasize again that masks were not a significant feature of Siberian ritual attire, in sharp contrast to the practices of the neighboring Yup'ik Eskimos, the Alaskan maritime sea hunters just across the Bering Strait (see 2), who are discussed in Part II. This is particularly intriguing considering the almost completely parallel nature of Alaskan and Siberian shamanic beliefs: for both, a shaman's initial dismemberment, as well as his dramatic flights through the highest heavens and dangerous journeys to the deepest seas, were accepted dogma. It must be acknowledged, however, that the fringe of some Siberian shamans' headgear (see 1 and 30) presumably served much the same function as certain Alaskan masks: to hide the face of a practicing shaman and allow a patient's imagination to fill in details.

II

THE ARCTIC
AND ALASKA:
ESKIMO

*In traditional belief, attention and respect towards sea
mammals…are reciprocated by the animals' willing gift of
their lives and flesh. Songs, ritual and artistically embellished
weapons, boats, charms and clothing attract the animals
and express this human esteem.*

—

Aron L. Crowell[1]

T he great wealth of ancient Alaska lay in its animals (38). Evidence reflecting belief in a collaborative reciprocity between the Arctic hunters and their marine prey provides the earliest traces that can be found of shamanic practices in the New World's Far North.[2] Such proof exists thanks to the deeply ingrained artistic sense of the Eskimo.[3] Edmund Carpenter, an anthropologist well versed in northern climes, was fascinated by the sensory relationships Arctic people had with their surroundings and how those sensitivities were traditionally revealed in their art: "Nowhere is life more difficult than in the Arctic, yet when life there is reduced to its basic essentials, art and poetry turned out to be among those essentials."[4]

Problems exist with determining exactly how the initial peopling of North America's Far North came about. It is generally accepted that those who came to inhabit the huge Arctic expanses were descendants of immigrants from Siberia, who were the first to master survival in the demanding northern lands. The Alaskan pioneers—archaeologists call them the Paleo-Eskimo—probably arrived about 5,000 years ago in one or more waves, *after* the initial groups of Siberian migrants who had continued south to populate the rest of North and South America.[5] There is little consensus about the duration or precise timing of the later Arctic migration; there is speculation, however, that their descendants include the "Dorset" people, named after their type site located on Canada's Cape Dorset (Map 4), and for whom the ancient record is more extensive than for most Arctic peoples.[6]

37 (opposite) John McIntyre's *Issiisaayuq* "contact" mask tells the story of an early shaman who foretold the coming of the first white people. A stylized ghost ship is depicted, which is said to have been followed in 1778 by the identical craft of Captain Cook, who sailed into the mouth of the Kuskokwim River to trade.

Map 4 (overleaf) The Alaskan sphere of the Far North.

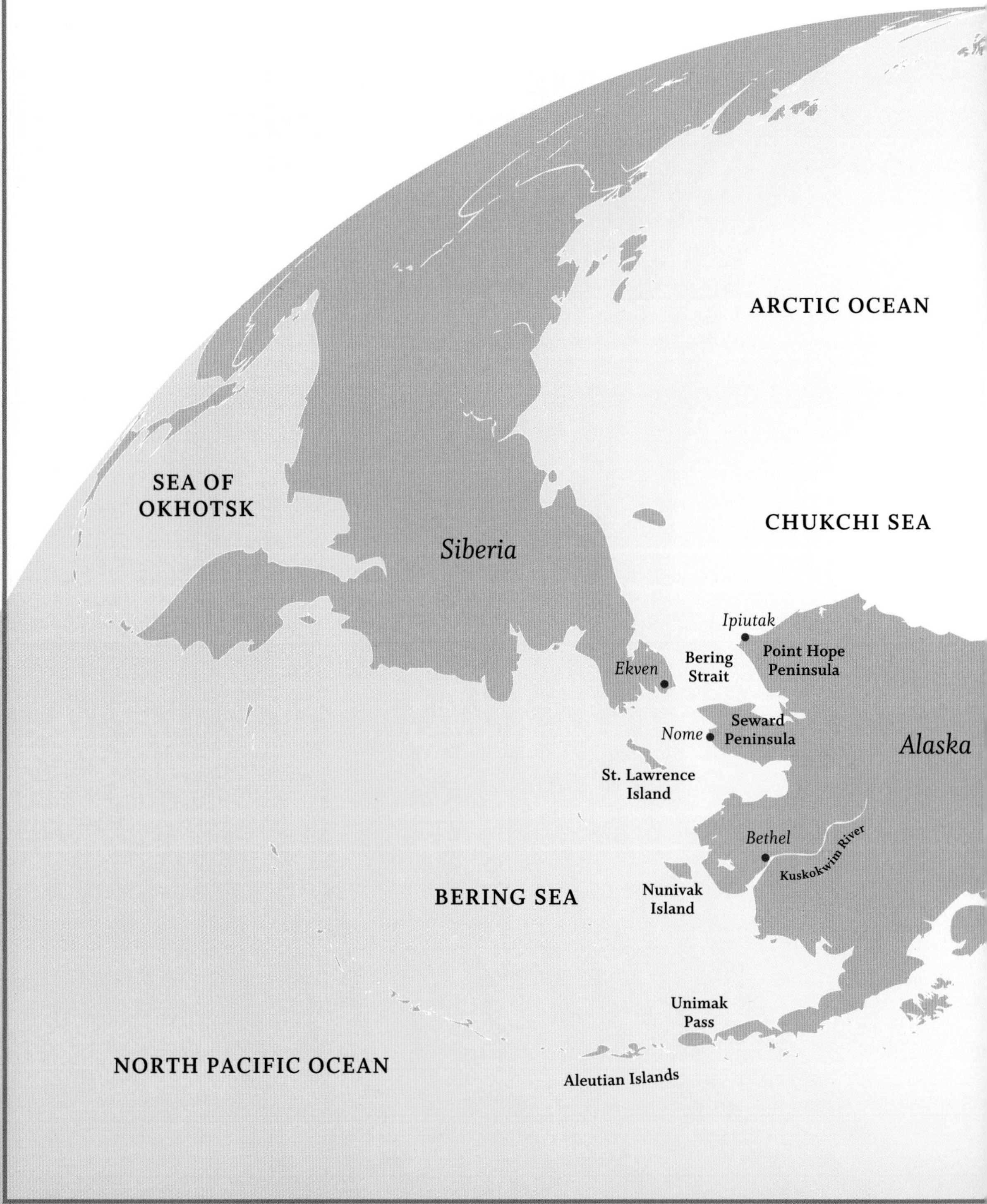

ARCTIC OCEAN

SEA OF OKHOTSK

CHUKCHI SEA

Siberia

Ipiutak

Bering Strait

Point Hope Peninsula

Ekven

Seward Peninsula

Nome

St. Lawrence Island

Alaska

Bethel

Kuskokwim River

BERING SEA

Nunivak Island

Unimak Pass

NORTH PACIFIC OCEAN

Aleutian Islands

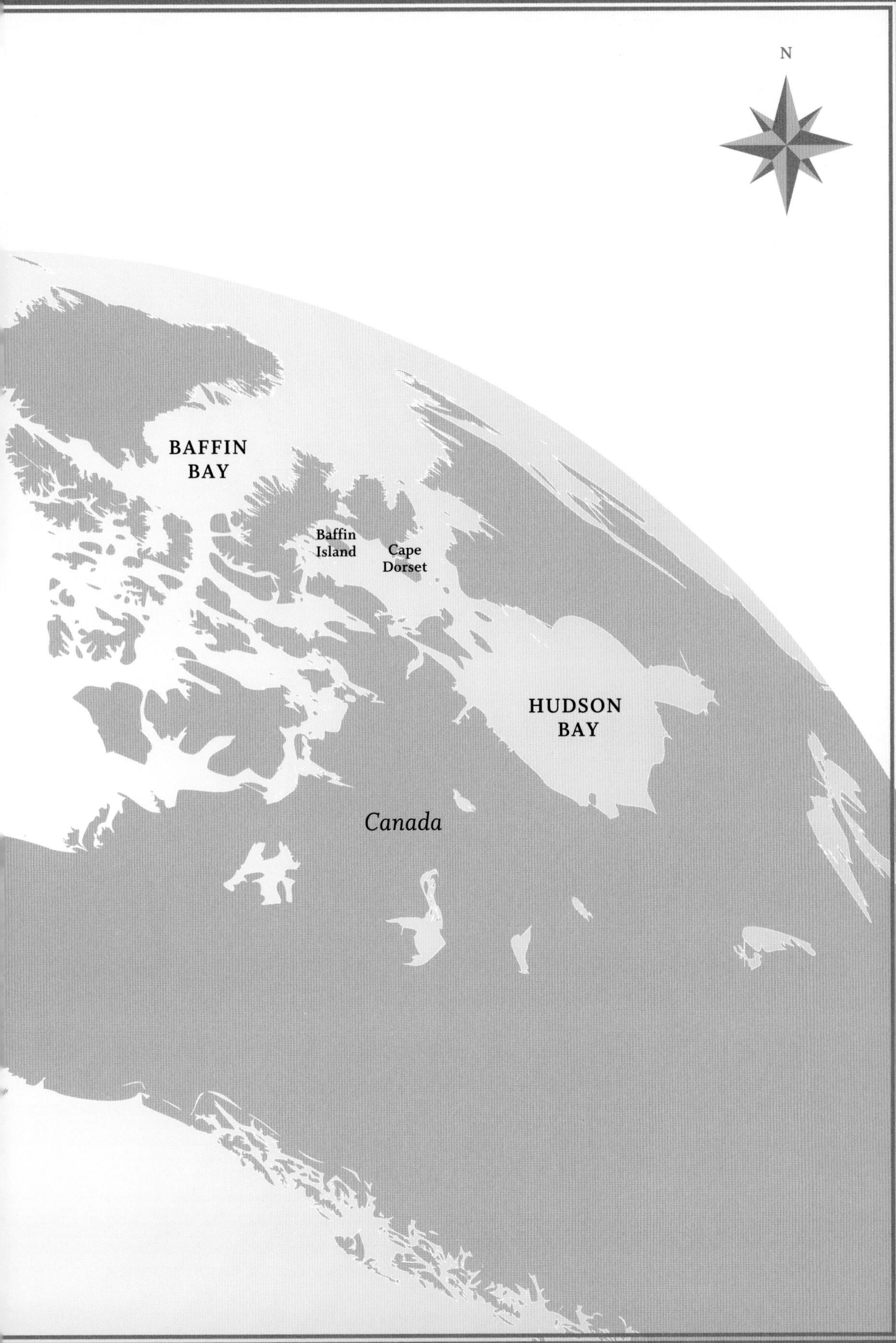

N

BAFFIN
BAY

Baffin
Island   Cape
           Dorset

HUDSON
BAY

Canada

38 (above) The great
wealth of Alaskan animals
includes not only the polar
bear and walrus, but also
a variety of seals, as well
as two whales, the huge
Gray whale and the elusive
Narwhal, particularly
valuable because of the
male's long, spiraling ivory
tusk. *Walruses/Polar Bear
Scene* by James Kivetoruk
Moses (1900–82).
Watercolor, 12 × 8"
(30 × 20 cm).

39 (opposite) This early,
Dorset-period (ca. 500 BC)
mask—which is the size of
a human face—displays
incised tattoo marks as
well as up-turned eyes.
(see 18). Height: 6⅝"
(17.5 cm).

THE DORSET PEOPLE

The culture now known as the Dorset slowly developed about
2,500 years ago; their surviving artifacts reflect a way of life that
was richer and more secure than that of the Paleo-Eskimo, but
nonetheless continued to be formidably demanding. Major adap-
tive problems had to be solved before any of the early migrants
could inhabit the North American Arctic, which required the
ability to survive long periods of intense cold, patchy and highly
seasonal food resources, and lack of a human support system.
The cultural solutions worked out over millennia involved the
invention of heat-saving, tailored fur clothing, the domestication of dogs for hauling belongings, including skin tents and
other household gear involved in a nomadic Arctic lifestyle, and
the perfection of skin-covered boats for hunting on icy seas. The
Dorset people also had to develop social behavior emphasizing
cooperation and sharing, as well as a lifestyle resulting in rapid
childhood learning of adult skills.

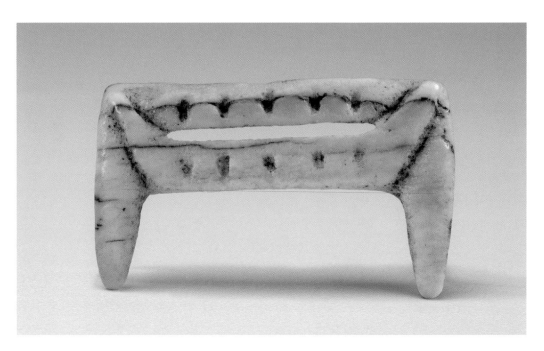

The extant carvings of the Dorset hunters reveal that they were vitally concerned with the relationship between humans and animals. That, in turn, suggests that they followed a shamanic religion in which all living creatures combined the physical and spiritual qualities of both humans and animals, postulating a distant past when there was no cognitive difference between any living creatures.

40 (opposite above) One of the ploys of shamans was to appear to go through a "transformation." This set of carved ivory teeth (ca. 500 BC) would assist a practitioner in his shapeshifting into a frightening predator such as a bear or wolf. Length 1⅛" (2.8 cm).

41 (opposite below) Just as shamans are sometimes drawn with their skeletons visible (see ill. 7) so, too, with depictions of shamans' spirit helpers, as is the case with this Dorset-period ivory carving of a swimming polar bear decorated with skeletal markings. The skeleton was considered the seat of the soul in all creatures. Length 5⅜" (13.8 cm).

Many of the carvings made by Dorset artists seem to have been used in religious practices, and may have been the tools and instruments of shamans in visiting and manipulating the world of the spirits...[Among those extant artifacts are] life-sized masks [3] carved from driftwood, painted with red ochre and enlivened with incised tattoo lines.[7]

There are two forms of these Dorset masks. The eyes of some masks turn up, while the eyes of others slant down, giving each face either a distinctively good-natured expression or a depressed countenance. They may represent mythological personages, or perhaps they contrast the stereotyped dispositions of males and females. The tradition of depicting these contrasting happy/sad faces has survived in certain present-day Yup'ik regalia (see 56).

Evidence of early shamanic practices involving human-animal transformations appears in a carved ivory set of animal teeth with long projecting canines, like those of such predators as bears or wolves (40). It is believed that this Dorset-period piece was meant to be placed in front of the mouth, gripped by clenched teeth, and thus give the impression of a human face in the process of transformation.[8]

Many of the Dorset animal carvings represent spirit helpers and hence were probably amulets that made up part of a shaman's equipment. A case in point is a replica of a swimming polar bear (41). A clue that this carving is not intended to represent an actual bear but rather an animal spirit—perhaps a specific shaman's helper spirit—is suggested by the skeletal markings on the back and sides of the piece. In shamanic thought, the skeleton, as seen through the skin, symbolizes the seat of the soul, as both skin and skeleton outlast the soft flesh of the body.

42 (opposite) This tiny Dorset-period ivory masquette, with its intriguing animal-like "ears," is so small that it—together with the shamanic mask shown in 43—could easily fit on a human palm, with room to spare. Height 1⅜" (3.5 cm).

In Dorset art, representations of humans are less common than those of polar bears, but are found in forms that imply something other than simple portraits. For example, one ivory masquette (42) depicts a serene human face, but the concave upper edge of the mask suggests a hint of animal ears. An unexplained aspect of many of these ancient carvings is their tiny size. Were they so minute because they were worn close to the body as protective amulets, by a people constantly on the move? Perhaps a clue as to their range of use exists in carvings coming from later cultures where similar-sized pieces appear to have adorned shamanic costumes.

EARLY ESKIMO

The first major florescence of the Eskimo way of life, found on St. Lawrence Island and north along the nearby Siberian and Alaskan coasts, was what scholars call the Old Bering Sea Culture I,[9] dated to 200 BC through AD 100. Ekven is one of the largest archaeological sites located on the Siberian side of the Bering Sea, near Cape Dezhnev. From an Ekven burial dating to Old Bering Sea Culture II (AD 100–300), comes a carved walrus-ivory piece that is clearly religious in nature: a miniature, anthropomorphic sculpture in the form of a tiny shamanic mask (43). Judging from holes on the top of this carving, it may have been sewn onto a garment.[10] There is supporting evidence for such a practice from an analogous archaeological site, one located on the Bering Strait's Alaskan shore.

43 From the site of Ekven, located on the Siberian side of the Bering Strait, comes a tiny, walrus-ivory mask that includes small holes along the top, suggesting it was once sewn onto a shaman's costume. Height 1½" (3.8 cm).

Ipiutak, which sits at the far tip of the Point Hope Peninsula in northwest Alaska, was inhabited from 100–200 BC to around AD 800. Among other items found at this important site are shamanic grave goods including animal carvings and chains (44). The latter are similar to the metal adornments that were attached to Siberian shamans' costumes; iron chains and stylized animal figures appear most frequently on those garments (see Part I, ills 22–26). The Siberian pieces were all composed of metal, but without sufficient metal the Ipiutak shamans substituted

44 Shamans at Ipiutak, a site located on the Alaskan side of the Bering Strait, were obviously impressed by the metal-adorned shamanic attire of their Siberian neighbors. Sections of ivory chains were the Alaskans' response to that sartorial challenge. Length 15½" (39.5 cm).

walrus ivory—their precious material—in imitation of the impressive Siberian iron adornments.[11] Shamanic activity at Ipiutak is further confirmed by a group of tiny, grotesquely shaped human heads carved of ivory or antler (45) that were probably inserted into sticks and then used in healing, divination, or prognosticating rituals.

An ancient carving of a shamanic transformation (46) has survived from a site in the Bering Strait area that dates to the early Thule period (ca. AD 1000–1600). This moose bone or sea ivory sculpture depicts the body of a Bowhead whale with a human head. The figure—which also resembles a seal when viewed from the side—may have been a hunter's or, perhaps, a shaman's charm (*qaagliniq*) whose purpose was to attract animals. The attachment holes on the side of the piece may indicate that the carving also had a functional use, possibly as a drum handle or fishing implement.

Aron L. Crowell, an authority on such ancient ivories of the Bering Strait area, states:

> From the Old Bering Sea (OBS) era to the present day, Bering Strait art
> and ceremony have expressed metaphysical concepts of reciprocity and
> transformation. These ideas permeate interaction between humans and
> whales, polar bears, walruses, and seals, which provide nearly the whole
> basis of survival in the Arctic maritime environment. In traditional belief,
> attention and respect toward these sea mammals and their person-like
> inner spirits (Yup'ik *yua*, Inupiaq *inua*, "its person") are reciprocated by the
> animals' willing gift of their lives and flesh. Song, ritual, and artistically
> embellished weapons, boats, charms, and clothing attract the animals and
> express this human esteem.[12]

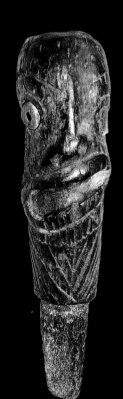

45 From the Alaskan site of Ipiutak—located at the far end of the Point Hope Peninsula—comes a group of tiny, grotesque human heads. Their construction indicates that they were probably attached to the end of sticks, so as to be visible in the course of a shamanic ritual. Heights from 1³⁄₈" (3.5 cm) to 2⁵⁄₈" (6.8 cm).

46 (above) Depictions of shamans in the act of transformation are particularly powerful (see 20). This small ivory carving of a Bowhead whale with a human head has caught the practitioner in the act of shapeshifting into a completely different mammalian form. Length 3" (7.6 cm).

47 (opposite) Embedded on the obverse side of the wooden Gray whale (see 49) is a carved-ivory shaman's tattooed face.

Obviously, the ancient Eskimos viewed the relationship between humans and animals as one of interdependence. Further, some Natives still contend that when the sea mammals are not hunted they feel neglected and hence decline. Crowell quotes a woman as saying, "If you don't hunt them, they will just go down, dying, but if we can hunt them they'll multiply. That's what we Eskimos believe."[13]

Further evidence of the strong connection between shamans, hunters, and their marine prey exists on a late 19th-century wooden carving of a Gray whale (47, 49) whose meticulous detailing conforms in every way to the huge beast upon which it is based (48). This exceptional piece no doubt served as a whale charm used by hunters when pursuing such

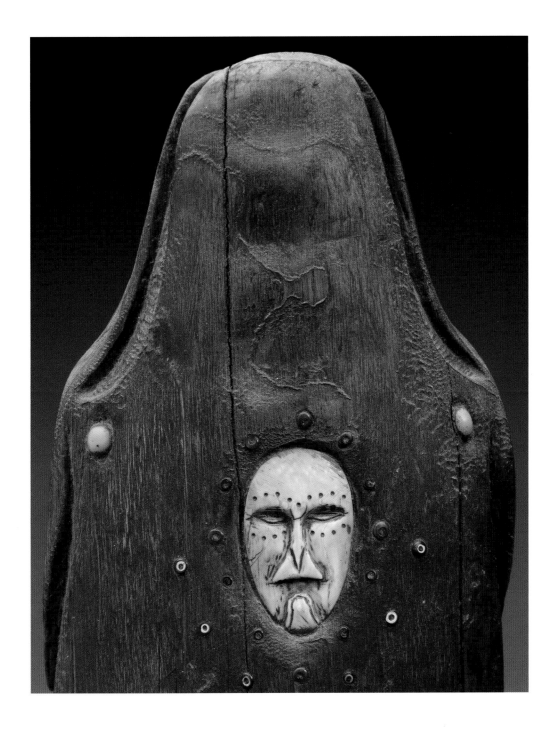

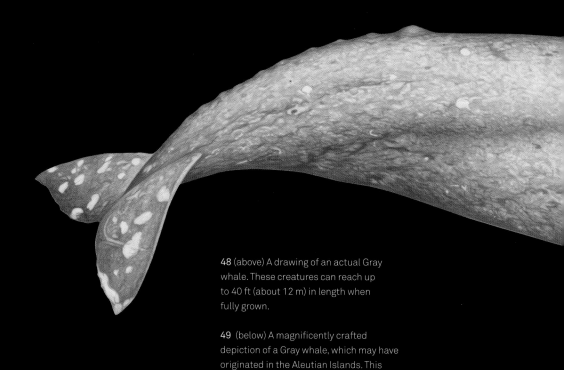

48 (above) A drawing of an actual Gray whale. These creatures can reach up to 40 ft (about 12 m) in length when fully grown.

49 (below) A magnificently crafted depiction of a Gray whale, which may have originated in the Aleutian Islands. This wooden carving reproduces in accurate detail one of the most far-ranging of Earth's mammals. Length 12¼" (31 cm).

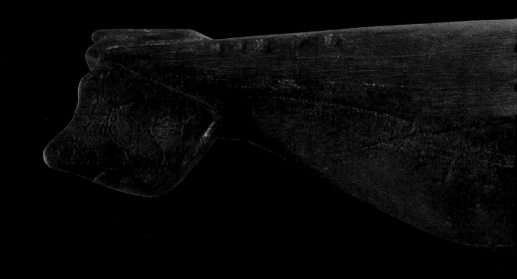

behemoths in their fragile, skin-covered boats, called *umiaks*, which hold
several men. Bowhead and Gray whales were the focus of Bering Sea and
Chukchi Sea *umiak* whaling because they were slow-swimming and relatively docile, making an approach by crews of paddling or sailing boats possible.
Gray whales winter in lagoons off Baja California and Mexico and then
travel north along the coast of western North America in the spring.[14] Their
route takes them through Unimak Pass at the eastern end of the Aleutian
Island chain and then on into the rich feeding grounds of the Bering and
Chukchi Seas. All that is known about the wooden Gray whale (see 49),
which comes from a private collection, is a worn sticker on the back that
reads, "*Isles Aleoutes Baleine de Schaman perles et os 1895.*" Such charms were
hung in the bow of the *umiak* to magically compel whales to draw near, and
often had their strength further enhanced by a quartz crystal placed into a
carving's obverse.[15] Note that into the wooden whale's upper side is inserted
an ivory shaman's tattooed face, which is carved with a memorably powerful
and commanding countenance (47).

ESKIMO PICTORIAL ART

The history of Eskimo artistic expression dates far back in time, as the
Dorset-period, ca. 500 BC, carvings demonstrate (see 39–42). Eventually,
this tradition also came to include pictorial art. In 1778, Captain Cook collected the first documented drill bow handle along the Bering Strait (50).[16]
On it are engraved pictorial scenes, narratives of Native life depicting an
array of Eskimo vignettes. The American side of the Bering Strait is the
Seward Peninsula, a land mass that juts out from the coast of Alaska to
within 55 miles (88 km) of Siberia's East Cape, across open sea. Drill bows
depicting complicated pictorial narratives were often produced on the
Seward Peninsula, homeland of the Inupiaq Eskimo. The Inupiaq are an
unusually artistic group, exhibiting acute powers of both initial observation
and subsequent reproduction, skills that proved to be particularly suited to
making accurate drawings of their surroundings. The Inupiaq artists and the

materials needed for their historical documentations were brought together as the result of a White Man's calculating experiment that went awry.

In the 1890s, attempts were made to introduce domestic reindeer breeding into Alaska, together with an education system. The establishment of Alaskan Territorial schools to aid the spread of Christian missionization, together with instruction in reindeer herding, were intimately intertwined during the period from 1892 into the 1920s. The reindeer plan was to serve as a strategy to Christianize Alaskan Natives by altering their traditional, subsistence-based lifestyle and thus make it possible to resettle them in key communities. The long-range plan was doomed from the beginning. First, experienced herders were needed to teach the Alaskans how to care for the tame reindeer. Initially, Siberian Chukchi were chosen but since they were traditional enemies of their Alaskan Inupiaq neighbors just across the Bering Strait, that choice was destined to fail. Nor did the importation of Lapland reindeer herders fare better.

Although reindeer were originally touted as substitutes for sled dogs, as well as a commercial source of meat, over time reindeer did not prove nearly as hardy as sled dogs (51), and lobbyists for Western ranchers in the Lower 48 states argued convincingly against reindeer meat serving as a beef substitute. As for the Inupiaq themselves, they came to distrust the entire reindeer-herding enterprise. To them the tame reindeer looked exactly like wild caribou—a much desired food source—but government regulations forbade the killing and consumption of the reindeer, and Alaskan herders were punished when they transgressed. For the Eskimo, who were by nature and nurture hunters, and had been for millennia, to be converted to a lifetime of guarding, protecting, and cosseting a food source simply was not in their DNA.[17]

Nonetheless, the ill-fated Christian missionization scheme did serve to introduce the young hunters to pencils and paper on which to draw, as well as exposing them to illustrated magazines. The result is a treasure trove of Eskimo drawings. The Inupiaq artists depicted the world around

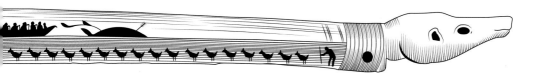

50 (above and opposite) A drill bow, collected during Captain James Cook's 1778 expedition to the Bering Strait area, displays pictorial scenes of Eskimo life.

them, which fortunately included activities of local shamans, as depicted in the drawing of *The Great Medicine Man* (53).

However, according to one Inupiaq drawing (54), shamanic intervention was not necessary to bring about an unusual event. In June 1948, the hunter James Kivetoruk Moses—one of the most acclaimed of Inupiaq painters—stated that he had seen an unclothed woman sitting on the edge of a large ice pack. To add credence to his account, Kivetoruk Moses, a respected man not given to hyperbole, lists the names of his fellow hunters who also claimed to have seen the naked lady.[18] Happily, surprising events may still occur in the Far North.

The Seward Peninsula Inupiaq, in their 19th- and 20th-century drawings, depict the here-and-now world around them whereas their southern neighbors, the Yup'ik artists of the Bering Sea coast, were more concerned with the spiritual world, as expressed not only in their creative masks and ceremonial paraphernalia, discussed below, but also in a rare set of Yup'ik drawings. These unusual sketches were created as the result of a serendipitous meeting between a knowledgeable collector, Knud Rasmussen, and a group of Yup'ik-speaking Eskimo from Nunivak Island.

We are beholden to the fieldwork of Knud Rasmussen (1933–79) for much of our knowledge of Alaskan ritual regalia. He was a Greenlander, a polar explorer, and an anthropologist, the son of a Danish missionary and an Inuit-Danish mother. Although he led a number of expeditions, his greatest achievement was regarded as the Fifth Thule Expedition (1921–24), which

51 (above) In an attempt to introduce domestic reindeer breeding into Alaska, reindeer were touted as substitutes for sled dogs. The plan did not work out, as the Inupiaq artist Etoachima—who may appear in this drawing—illustrates vividly in this weary scene.

52 (opposite) A drawing made in Nome, Alaska, in 1924 for Knud Rasmussen by a Yup'ik artist from Nunivak Island. It depicts the sea lion, in myth the most ancient of sea mammals. The encompassing "circle of the world" visualizes the spirit's unborn brood.

was designed to investigate the origin of the Eskimo race.[19] A team of seven explorers first went to eastern Arctic Canada where they began collecting specimens and taking interviews, as well as excavating. Rasmussen subsequently left that team and traveled by dog-sled for sixteen months with two Inuit hunters across North America to Nome, Alaska. He then tried to continue on into Russia; but his visa was refused. Rasmussen was the first European to cross the Northwest Passage by dog-sled.

In 1924, while Rasmussen was in Nome—then the largest trading center in all of northwest Alaska—he discovered that a group of Yup'ik-speaking Eskimos from Nunivak Island was there, to serve as witnesses in the murder trial of an accused shaman. Rasmussen, who was eager to gather as much information as possible regarding Nunivak ceremonial artifacts, set about interviewing the visiting islanders with particular emphasis on obtaining sketches of their ritual regalia. This was a very provident move because those drawings (52) were made

53 (overleaf) The Alaskan Inupiaq artists of the Seward Peninsula painted the world around them. This scene of a shaman summoning two spirits to report on his missing sons is by James Kivetoruk Moses. Note the shaman's tonsured head, his labret, fur parka and pants, and the daily life objects in his hut.

at a time when the Eskimo mask festivals and traditional hunting methods were still a living reality on Nunivak Island. The information Rasmussen recorded regarding the Nunivak artists' drawings and carved wooden objects reflected a strong influence from the Russian Orthodox Mission on the Asian mainland opposite Nunivak Island.[20] It is also interesting that one ambitious local shaman was quite willing to convert to Christianity if it would prove advantageous to his shamanic calling.[21]

54 (pages 98–99) An Eskimo
mermaid sitting on the
edge of a large piece of
floating sea ice in the spring
of 1948, illustrated by the
accomplished Inupiaq artist,
James Kivetoruk Moses (see
page 93).

55 (opposite) A Yup'ik full-
face Swan Mask, "which
depicts a shaman's helping
spirit that brings swans,
geese, ducks and other birds
back to the coast in the
springtime to provide the
people with nourishment"
(Bolz and Sanner 1999: 216).
Height 33" (84 cm).

MASKING TRADITIONS

When considering Eskimo masking traditions, the
costuming practices of the mainland Yup'ik are particularly illustrative because this coastal Bering Sea culture
is among the most artistic of all of the historic Eskimo
groups.[22] The Yup'ik traditional homeland is the Yukon-
Kuskokwim region, a lowland delta the size of Kansas.
The region's population of more than 23,000 (the largest
Native population in Alaska) lives scattered among fifty-
six villages ranging from 200 to 1,000 people each. The
regional center is Bethel, with a population of nearly 7,000
people.[23]

In the Yup'ik areas, shamans and their helpers made the
cosmos' unseen forces visible through a dramatic use of a
variety of masks: for example, full-faced masks (55), small
finger masks (56), forehead masks (57), and shamanic masks (58). It was
during the winter that many of the Yup'ik's great annual ceremonies were
held. Three were of particular importance: the Bladder Festival, honoring
the souls of seals killed the previous year; the Feast of the Dead, honoring
recently deceased humans; and the dramatic Agayuyaraq Festival,[24] held to
invite animal spirits into the human world where they were made visible via
masked dances (59). The purpose of this ceremony was to please the helper
spirits of those animals still to be caught, in order to ensure the future needs
of the hunters who depended upon them.

In preparation for Agayuyaraq, a shaman oversaw the construction of the
elaborate masks through which the spirits were made manifest; the carvers
produced each piece according to the shaman's specification and each was
supposed to be used only once. These powerful masks—both inherently
dangerous and potentially beneficial—had to be handled carefully at all
times. Prior to use, they were hidden so as to protect them from human
gaze, lest the animals in question be offended.

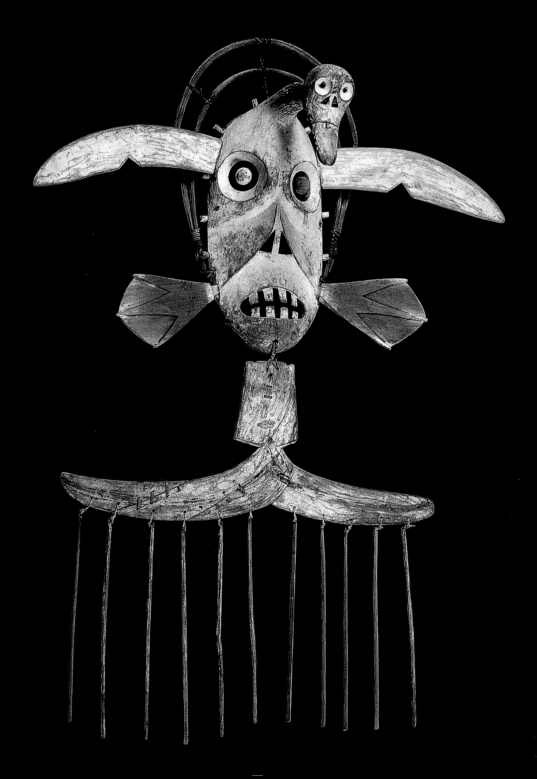

56 Twin Yup'ik finger masks depicting a male happy face and a female sad face. Height (of each) 3½" (9.2 cm).

57 A diving loon forehead mask from St. Michael, collected by Sheldon Jackson in 1892. The loon's *yua*, its inner spirit, is indicated by its human arms and legs. The thin rods encircling the upper half of the body may indicate the loon's ability to move between worlds. Length 31½" (80 cm).

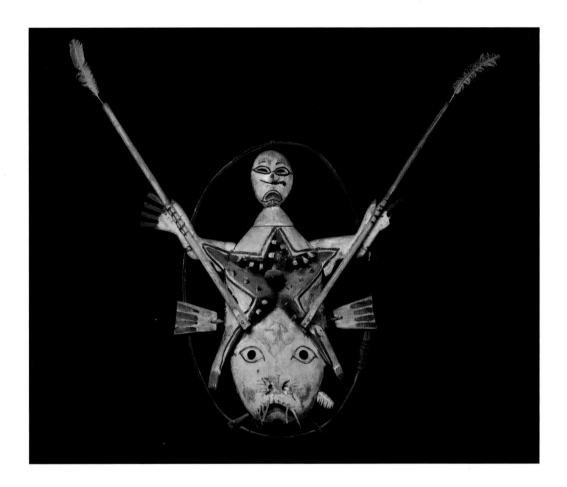

58 (above) A Yup'ik monumental dance mask depicts a shaman's journey to the spirit world in search of good fortune for his people in the coming year. The upper portion of the mask reveals a shaman with his raised arms grasping two long sticks, like harpoons, in his thumbless hands; his body is open to display a toothy interior. Height 35" (88.9 cm).

Following the Agayuyaraq ceremony, the masks were said to have been destroyed, either buried, burned, or placed far out on the tundra to rot. While that may have been the stated ideal, it does not appear always to have been the actual practice, given the quantity of masks still in existence.[25]

Yup'ik masks, which continue to play an important role in the culture, can be divided into two categories: the secular and the spiritual. Apropos of the latter, shamanic practitioners often wore masks known as *nepcetaq*, "the

59 A walrus mask made in 1946 in the remote coastal community of Qissunaq, an isolated area where, into the 1940s, the men still danced in the masks that they themselves had carved. Width 6" (15.2 cm).

60 (below) A shaman's *nepcetaq* mask, "one that sticks to the face." These important masks were worn primarily in performances, during visions, and while carrying out healing rituals. Height 24" (61 cm).

ones that stick to the face."[26] Used primarily in shamanic performances involving visions, *nepcetaq* masks (60) were additionally worn by shamans while performing healing and prognosticating rituals.

In contrast, secular masks were and are danced as part of the important festivals. For the Yup'ik, dancing is a form of praying so that the desired animals will respond when Eskimo hunters set off in pursuit. This type of dancing—which the men perform partly on their knees (61) to the beat of shallow, tambourine-like drums (62)—is a tradition reaching far back into

prehistoric times, and is claimed by the Natives to have continued unchanged from its original form. As a result, contemporary Yup'ik dancing is considered a living link to the past, wherein younger community members bring to life old songs and stories (63). In this context, each Yup'ik mask is integral to the telling of a particular tale (37).[27]

In the words of Paul John, Toksook Bay, April 15, 1994:

61 (above) Male Yup'ik dancers performing on their knees while posing with a "set" of three unmatched masks. The exact place and date of this photo is not given.

> The tradition of dance in its many forms was a uniting force...Gathering for dancing often enabled distant family members to meet each other, in many cases for the first time. For a long time this tradition, based on our longstanding value system of compassion and love for each other, has been a system for perpetuating kinship, ties.[28]

62 A Yup'ik drum with a carved shaman serving as the drum's handle. Note that the practitioner's body has been opened to expose his ribs and organs, a reflection of the shaman's traumatic mythological initiation. Diameter 19½" (49.5 cm); handle 15½" (38.7 cm).

SHAMANIC REGALIA AND WESTERN ART

Although Dorset-period archaeological pieces dating from 2,500 years ago suggest that early Arctic peoples may have decorated their shamanic costumes in a Siberian manner, by the 20th century the area's shamans—like all of the Eskimo peoples—wore climate-appropriate fur parkas and

63 (above) John McIntyre dancing on his knees; among the Yup'ik, dancing is a form of praying to the needed animals to ask for their cooperation with Eskimo hunters.

pants (see 51, 53, 63), survival apparel. The shamanic aspect of their attire was limited to full-face masks, forehead masks, finger masks and drums, some with carved shamanic handles (see 62).

The impact of the dramatic Yup'ik masks was to have a far-reaching influence on Western art. This came about, indirectly, as the result of the efforts of an Alaskan trader who established himself in Bethel, in the Kuskokwim Valley, in 1905: Adams Hollis Twitchell. Twitchell collected significant groups of Yup'ik ceremonial masks from the region, and made the extra effort to record

64 (opposite) One of the twelve weather-related masks: Oangiluk, the rain spirit who brings warm weather. Twitchell (quoted by Donald Ellis in 2011) states, "the mask represents the rain spirit that brings warm weather... when the wind strikes him in the rear, he [responds happily], and as the wind and rain pass through him they become warm and mild. The wind passes through the large tube." Height 34" (86.4 cm).

65 (right) One of the twelve weather-related masks collected by Twitchell: Negakfok, "the cold weather spirit." Perhaps this spirit is so glum because spring is soon to follow. Height 35¾" (91 cm).

66 An asymmetrical pair of masks collected by Sheldon Jackson in 1893. Many Yup'ik masks were created in just such a dual format but subsequently were separated when one was sold singly. Heights 20⁴/₅" (52.8 cm) and 24¹/₁₀" (61.3 cm).

the original Yup'ik names and stories associated with some. This detailed information proved particularly illuminating in the case of twelve outstanding weather-related masks, some beneficent (64), others not so much so (65).

By 1916, Twitchell had collected a highly important group of fifty-five Yup'ik masks, which he sold to George Gustav Heye, who had just established his new Museum of the American Indian, Heye Foundation, in New York.²⁹ Unfortunately, by the early 1940s Heye, experiencing financial difficulties, began selling works from his museum. Often, those sales involved one of an associated pair, for many Yup'ik masks were created in a dual format (66).

67 A Yup'ik mask from Alaska's Nunivak Island
embodies the Yup'ik theme of duality. Here a shaman's
transformation is dramatically conveyed in the design
of two identities depicted in one: that of a man and
that of a fox. The two surrounding rings represent the
dual worlds of human and animal spirits; the light and
dark color scheme further emphasizes the concept
of duality (Ellis 2011: 30). Height 13" (33 cm).

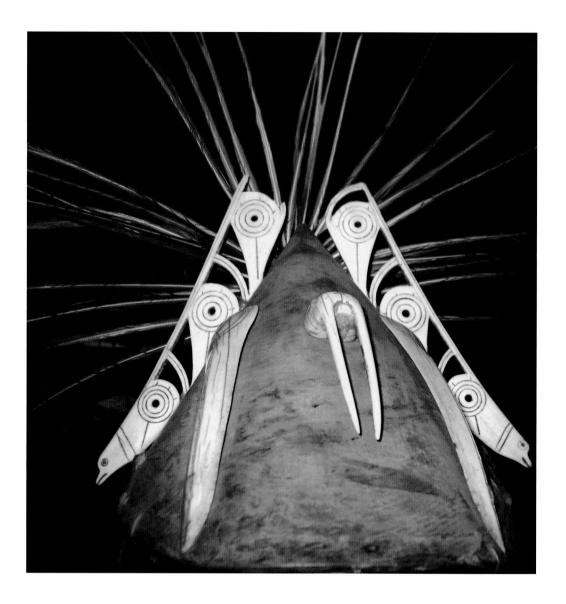

68 (above) A decorated Eskimo bentwood hunting hat. 12½ × 9" (31.74 × 22.86 cm).

69 (opposite) A drawing of an Eskimo hunter wearing a decorated, bentwood hunting hat while scouting marine animals in Alaska's Far North.

In the early 1940s, the antiquarian Julius Carlebach acquired a group of twenty-six remarkable masks from the Heye Foundation, pieces that had been collected originally by Twitchell in the Kuskokwim River area. Carlebach had an antique store on Third Avenue in New York, which became a meeting place for a group of Surrealist artists and intellectuals who had fled Europe during the Second World War. Max Ernst, having discovered a carved Haida spoon in the window in 1941, returned often, bringing André Breton, Kurt Seligmann, Marcel Duchamp, Yves Tanguy, Roberto Matta, and Enrico Donati.[30] The influential French Structuralist, Claude Lévi-Strauss, was also deeply impressed with the Yup'ik masks,[31] although his primary attraction was to the Tlingit material from the Northwest Coast.

The Surrealists and European intellectuals were among the first to recognize Yup'ik masks as exceptionally refined works of art. The influence of such complex and sophisticated pieces (67) on the evolution of Western art must not be underestimated.[32]

In sum, the impressive Yup'ik masks reflect a subsistence-oriented culture dependent on a hunter-prey collaborative relationship involving a profound respect for each animal's spirit. Wherever possible, the Alaskan maritime hunters of the Far North honored the sea mammals not only through the use of elaborate masks and impressive dancing, but also by wearing highly decorated hunting gear—including intricately shaped, bentwood hunting hats (68)—based on the premise that beauty drew game (69). Judging from an ancient, 1,500-year-old archaeological carving of a "reverently clad" marine hunter (70), this custom had existed in the Far North for a very long time.

Although most Europeans in the Far North during the early historical period seem to have been blinded by their own cultural prejudices to the wonders they witnessed, at least one had open eyes. Martin Sauer, a member

70 An ancient walrus-ivory carving of a kayaker wearing a decorated, bentwood hunting hat, ca. AD 500–1200, St. Lawrence Island. Height 1⅝" (4.5 cm).

of the Billings Expedition sent to northern Russia and America by Russia's Catherine II in 1785–94, wrote:

The capacity of the natives of these islands [the Aleutians] infinitely surpasses every idea that I had formed of the abilities of savages....Their behavior...is not rude or barbarous, but mild, polite, and hospitable. At the same time, the beauty, proportion, and art with which they make their boats, instruments, and apparel evince that they by no means deserve to be termed stupid; an epithet so liberally bestowed upon those who Europeans call savage.[33]

III

THE TLINGIT Of THE NORTHWEST COAST

*In 1744, when Europeans first encountered the Northwest
Coast cultures, they discovered what experts William Fitzhugh
and Aron Crowell refer to as "the most stylistically complex
art of any of the hunting and fishing peoples of the Americas...
based on the conventionalization of distinctive features of
animals, often represented in humanoid form."*

✳

A nd now it is time to speak of the Tlingit, the northernmost of the dramatic Northwest Coast cultures.

The narrow, island-fringed coastal strip that stretches from southern Alaska down through British Columbia (Map 5) is geographically as impressive as the late 18th-/early 19th-century Indian groups that inhabited it. To the west, a rugged range of precipitous mountains plunges almost directly into the Pacific, where cold Arctic waters mix with the warm Japanese current to produce a mild but damp climate of lingering fogs and abundant rainfall, an environment that has created a rainforest with dense stands of fir, hemlock, and cedar (72). Appropriately, the region's art and architecture featured wood.

In the winter, the Northwest Coast peoples lived in permanent villages marked by cedar-plank clan houses and towering, heraldic house poles (73); they also hollowed out the loftiest of the red cedars to create large traveling and war canoes (74, 75)[1] enhanced with canoe prow figureheads (76). In this region of indented shorelines, myriad islands and steep impenetrable forests, boats offered the easiest means of transportation. Moreover, neither the dense forests nor the steep mountain ranges hindered trade because the Indians traveled widely in smaller dug-out canoes.[2]

The famous Northwest Coast artistic world was inhabited by the Nuu-chah-nulth (formerly known as Nootka), the

71 (opposite) A group of Tlingit Indians gathered in Sitka on December 9, 1904, for a potlatch. Among their prestigious costumes are two valuable Chilkat blankets and two prestigious high-crown hats woven of split spruce root. The wide-brimmed hat on the right has three rings; they may represent the owner's former potlatches. The center hat, worn with a Hudson Bay button blanket, displays a heraldic clan emblem and two rings. Many of the surrounding group are attired in intricately beaded and/or appliquéd clothing, as well as ceremonial headgear, nose rings, and face paint.

72 (overleaf) A photograph of a section of the Northwest Coast, showing Tlingit fishing platforms located on the Chilkat River.

73 (pages 124–125) A
portion of a Northwest
Coast village with cedar-
plank clan houses and
heraldic house poles.

Map 5 (opposite) The
Northwest Coast, showing
the borders of Alaska and
British Columbia as well
as the boundaries of
the region's principal
cultural groups.

Kwakwaka' wakw (formerly Kwakiutl), the Nuxalk (formerly Bella Coola), as well as the Tsimshian, the Haida, and the Tlingit (see Map 5). Although these peoples spoke different languages, they shared a common coastal culture—with subtle differences—dependent on marine resources. In that world of Nature's bounty, there was no agriculture, and neither room nor need for it. The diet was largely one of animal fats, thanks to abundant supplies of salmon and other fish (see 72). Some Northwest Coast groups were also whale hunters, hence whale as well as fish oil was available. So much oil was used that certain inner waterways were known as "grease trails."[3]

In 1741, when Europeans first encountered the Northwest Coast cultures, they discovered what the experts William W. Fitzhugh and Aron Crowell refer to as "the most stylistically complex art of any of the hunting and fishing peoples of the Americas. [This] art was based on the conventionalization of distinctive features of animals, often represented in humanoid form" (77).[4]

Several of the Northwest Coast groups had particular artistic specialties: the Haida were known for their complex, memorial house poles (see 73, 77), the Tsimshian for their imaginative amulets and soul catchers (78), and the Tlingit for the elegance of their formline (see 75). As the Northwest Coast specialist Bill Holm explains, the formline is:

> …a broad, line-like stroke—most often painted black—which delineates
> the main features of the creature being depicted. Formlines vary in width
> according to set principles and create design units that are joined in a
> continuous network across the design field. Joining these primary black
> formlines, and filling in many of the remaining spaces, are secondary
> formlines in red.[5]

Unlike many hunting and fishing cultures worldwide, the basic units of Northwest Coast political, social, and ceremonial life were not based on a

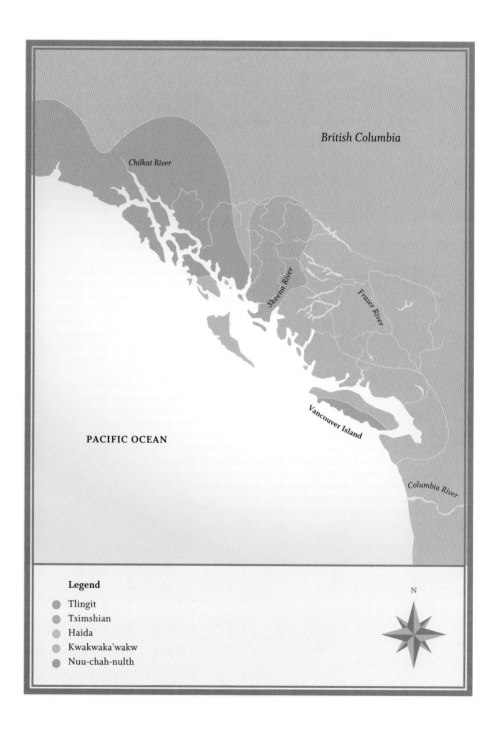

British Columbia

Chilkat River

Skeena River

Fraser River

Vancouver Island

PACIFIC OCEAN

Columbia River

Legend
- Tlingit
- Tsimshian
- Haida
- Kwakwaka'wakw
- Nuu-chah-nulth

N

74 (pages 128–129) A large traveling canoe, sails billowing, brings dancers to a feast. In 1988 Bill Holm, an authority on Northwest Coast cultures, explained their sails: "Everywhere on the coast (canoes) were sailed before the wind using sails of matting or thin planks. After European types of fore-and-aft sails of canvas were introduced in the late 18th century, Indians very successfully sailed their keelless canoes on points up to a beam reach, close to a right angle to the wind. Thereafter, most canoes of any size were equipped to step masts."

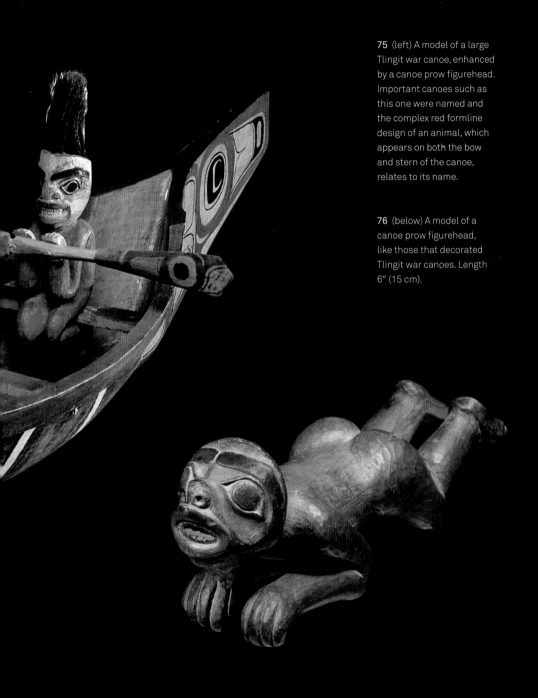

75 (left) A model of a large Tlingit war canoe, enhanced by a canoe prow figurehead. Important canoes such as this one were named and the complex red formline design of an animal, which appears on both the bow and stern of the canoe, relates to its name.

76 (below) A model of a canoe prow figurehead, like those that decorated Tlingit war canoes. Length 6" (15 cm).

77 A Haida house pole, an example of what William W. Fitzhugh and Aron Crowell call "the conventionalization of distinctive features of animals."

geographical region but rather on clan membership. To this day, when a Tlingit is asked his or her name, the proud reply is name, clan, and moiety, reminiscent of the inculcated response of a captured United States serviceman: name, rank, and serial number. With the Tlingit, however, such a prompt response is a matter of stating identity so that others will know if they are related. Relationship exchanges are very important in the Tlingit world.[6]

As the anthropologist Frederica de Laguna explains, "clans are divided into two sides or moieties, Ravens and Wolves (the latter called Eagles in the Tlingit far north)."[7] These are exogamous matrilineal groups, therefore serving as opposites so members can marry and perform ceremonial services for one another. Each moiety or side is composed of about sixty matrilineal clans, and each clan is composed of a variable number of house groups in different villages. The clan owns the most important forms of property: territories of hunting, fishing, and the collecting of wild foods. Their most precious possessions, however, were the totemic crests and ceremonial prerogatives vested in the clans and their lineages.[8] Indeed, among the Northwest Coast groups art was used to communicate social values through the display of a clan's heraldic insignia.

Because the Tlingit were skilled traders who also made maximum use of their bountiful environment, they acquired the excess wealth necessary to produce their own version of the famous Northwest Coast potlatches,

the region's renowned give-away celebrations. The great Tlingit potlatches would often last a week or more.

> During this time the families of the host clan would serve their high-ranking guests great feasts day after day in the large cedar-planked ceremonial houses. Guests were also witness to ceremonial transfers of traditional names and cultural privileges, such as the ownership of dances, masks, and ceremonial regalia. In a society of purely oral record-keeping, bearing witness to social transfers, marriages, and inheritances was extremely important, and the generosity of the hosts toward their guests served as a form of payment.[9]

78 A Tsimshian soul catcher. Bone pendants of this type were worn by shamans (see 100); their purpose was to hold the errant soul of an ill individual and then return it to the sick person in order to effect a cure. The soul of the ailing patient was blown back into his body through a soul catcher. This elaborate example depicts crouching bears at either end as well as a central splayed human figure. The Tsimshian are now believed to have produced all of the soul catchers used among the Northwest Coast cultures. Length 8¼" (20.9 cm).

The theatrical potlatches memorialized the Tlingit dead as well as maintained or elevated the rank of the still-living hosts, who were always arrayed in impressive attire (see 71). Nobility and rank were predominately displayed on the apparel and accoutrements of the Tlingit chiefs, who often wore prestigious Chilkat blankets (named for the Chilkat tribe located on the Chilkat River, 79),[10] together with spruce root hats ornamented with designs and attached carvings portraying animal totems ("crests"). Important outside contacts were reflected in exotic ornaments such as abalone-shell nose rings.

79 A prestigious Chilkat blanket, made of
mountain goat wool and shredded cedar bark.
Length 55¼" (140.3 cm), width 66½" (168.9 cm).

SHAMANS AND THEIR ROLE

In the world of the Northwest Coast cultures, all things—animals, birds, fish, insects, trees, plants, mountains, glaciers, winds, even the sea itself—were thought to possess souls or spirits. Since these spirits were more powerful than human beings, they had to be treated with great respect. Special rules existed for dealing with each species or being. For example, inasmuch as successful hunting and fishing entailed the killing of an animal, such an act was analogous to ending the life of a person. As a result, it was believed that a creature could only be taken if it permitted itself to be killed. Further, the dead animal had to be handled in a most respectful and special manner: no waste of an animal's flesh could be permitted.

And, of course, the world of spirits was the realm of shamans, whose role it was to maintain a harmonious balance between the amorphous spiritual beings and the all-too-vulnerable humans. Although all Northwest Coast cultures included shamans, it was among the Tlingit that shamanism was most pronounced.[11]

The Tlingit authority, Allen Wardwell, notes:

> To become a shaman, an individual must receive a sense of mystical vocation that marks him as a person possessing the unusual abilities a successful practitioner must have. These exceptional traits might be acquired through heredity and may be recognized at a young age, or they could come at any time during a person's life through exposure to spirit powers.[12]

Although women could become shamans, the Tlingit had such a strong taboo against menstrual fluids that women could only practice after menopause.[13] Even then, female shamans were never as powerful as their male counterparts. As for shamanic responsibilities, Aldona Jonaitis points out that it was the practitioners who were called on to "cure the sick, control the weather, accompany war parties, send spirits to spy on enemies, and ensure an abundance of fish and berries."[14] In short, each shaman was responsible for controlling any events caused by or related to supernaturals, as well as continually impressing an audience with the power of the shaman's spirits, and with his own abilities. It has been noted[15] that all of the ritual accoutrements used by the practitioners were actually of secondary importance to the dramatic impact of the shamanic séances themselves. The songs, chants, stories, and dances of those perform-ances were what most impressed those who were present:

> This practice was an extravaganza, beyond anything on this earth in
> its conception and acting, which we criticize but do not understand.
> The wild naked figure in all its contortions, with head thrown back
> and half-closed glazed eyes, flowing locks encircled in a cloud of down,
> the patient, the shadows cast by the fitful burning logs, the confusion
> of sounds, the atmosphere of smoke-dried salmon and human bodies,
> the tense expectancy of the crowd, all served to keep alive the belief
> in the unknown and in this juggler of life. When we consider that from
> childhood the Tlingit were reared in this atmosphere, is it any wonder
> that after a rudimentary education they should still revert to the past?[16]

The American who wrote that vivid, eye-witness account was a controver-sial individual involved in many facets of the late 19th-century Tlingit world, George Thornton Emmons (80).

Lieutenant George Thornton Emmons, United States Navy, one of the most knowledgeable authorities on Tlingit life, was stationed in Alaska during the 1880s and 1890s. During that period, the Navy was largely responsible for law and stability in the Territory. Emmons' duties brought him into close contact with the Tlingit, whose respect he won and whose culture he came to under-stand and hold in high regard. He came to comprehend Tlingit beliefs and values better than any of his contemporaries. Emmons also became a friend of many Tlingit leaders, traveled in their canoes, visited their homes,[17] recorded their traditions, was taken into one of their clans,[18] and regularly broke into their gravehouses to remove the valuable ritual paraphernalia they contained.

80 George Thornton
Emmons (1852–1945).

SHAMANIC REGALIA

The various objects of a shaman's professional attire could be made by the practitioner himself or by someone else according to his direction; however, until those objects were used by the shaman they contained no power. In the routine practices of all shamans, certain articles were considered necessary and hence were common to all practitioners, although none of those items were absolutely identical to one another. But there was one trait that defined all Tlingit shamans: long, tangled hair, purposefully uncombed, unwashed, and uncut (81).

Although various forms of ceremonial masks were worn in all Northwest Coast cultures, it was only among the Tlingit that practicing shamans wore masks,[19] some of which are true masterworks that aficionados rank among

81 (left) This photograph of a Tlingit shaman wearing a bear headdress was made in 1888, because the practitioner wanted his picture taken before he cut his long, tangled hair, which he believed would deprive him of his shamanic powers. Soon after this photograph was taken the shaman indeed did cut his hair, and then he died.

82 (opposite) One of the most outstanding and elegant of the Tlingit shamanic masks still extant represents the figure of an old woman. A frog emerges from her mouth and land otters are carved on her cheeks; on her forehead are eight land spirits with land otters on each side. Emmons collected this piece from a gravehouse in 1878 and describes it as the most elaborate Tlingit mask he had ever seen; he notes that it was a celebrated object among the people. Height 13" (33 cm).

the area's most prized artifacts (82). Emmons contended that such shamanic masks "exemplify the perfection of Tlingit art in carving. The realism of the features in their expression of feeling, the elaboration of ornamentation and the technical excellence of workmanship and finish gave [them] a superiority over all other masks of the Northwest Coast."[20]

Emmons also stated that "the mask…was the most important part of [any Tlingit] shaman's outfit. It alone represented the particular spirit [being summoned]… Every shaman had four masks representing the four spirits he controlled, but the most powerful shamans possessed eight spirits [and hence eight masks]."[21] Each mask was named for the spirit it represented and could be the face of a human (83), an animal, or part-human, part-animal (84). The wooden masks were usually painted, sometimes in a solid color, sometimes

83 (above) Emmons describes this mask as "the face of a dying man who has been killed in a fight with a knife," and adds that it was worn by a shaman impersonating the spirit of a warrior. Height 9⅝" (24.4 cm).

84 (opposite) Emmons described this mask as a sun dog spirit. Collected by Emmons in 1884–93 from the gravehouse of the shaman and chief of the Auk tribe, Kowee. Height 9¼" (23.5 cm).

85 (opposite) "Skun-doo," a celebrated shaman of the Wolf moiety of the Chilkoot clan. His hair was forcibly cut in 1888 so he had to renounce his profession, but later gave information to Emmons, and posed—presumably for a fee—for a photographer in 1894. He wears a feather headdress with a small round masquette at the front, a necklace of carved bones, a skin apron with rattling fringes, and carries a rattle in each hand.

86 (right and below) A shaman's oystercatcher rattle. On this example, the shaman is torturing a witch, whose head is thrown back. Length 13⅝" (34.6 cm).

in geometrical figures or in ceremonial designs in red, black, and blue-green; all paints were composed of native mineral colors. In addition to masks, a shaman's professional accoutrements (85) included one or more rattles, a skin waist apron, a bone necklace, a crown or headdress, and an assortment of amulets. Next to the mask, the most essential article used by a shaman was a wooden rattle. Each practitioner had one carved bird-type example, with a long neck and bill, which often represented an oystercatcher or raven (86). Often shamans also had a secondary rattle that was circular, oval, or cylindrical in shape, and frequently was carved (87).[22]

Typically, a shaman's deerskin apron (88) was painted to represent animal and supernatural figures and had a fringe at the bottom hung with puffin bills, deer dewclaws, or with bits of ivory that:

87 A Tlingit shaman's secondary rattle, carved with the face of a hawk. Height 8¾" (22.2 cm).

…bumped into each other during the shaman's dances and created a rhythmic music that complemented the percussive sounds of his drums and rattles and summoned the shaman's spirit helpers into their artistic images. This music harmonized with the sounds of the shaman's rattles, which also called his spirits.[23]

After trade with the Europeans had introduced brass thimbles, they sometimes were added to these aprons because of the tinkling noise they made when a shaman moved about. The apron was sometimes the only piece of clothing worn by a practitioner when holding a curing ceremony or séance (see 85).

A necklace of bone or ivory pendants (89) was a necessary ornament for every shaman. While some of the pendants were of bone, the finer ones were carved from walrus tusks, resulting in long, slender, beautifully polished rods of ivory.[24] The ivory rods or pendants were most likely imported from the Eskimo, because walrus are rarely seen south of the Alaska Peninsula. Further, certain of the ivory pieces often featured typical Eskimo incised designs, although others were clearly carved by the Tlingit.

There were three types of headdresses possessed by almost every practitioner. One was a crown of mountain goat horns (90) intended to represent bear claws; sometimes real bear claws were used, or wooden spikes shaped like horns. The second was an oblong hat of spruce root and colored grass stems woven in geometric designs (see 93). The third was a headdress in the shape of the ears of the brown bear, decorated with abalone squares, or made of shaped pieces of wood, hide, or copper, and then painted or etched and ornamented with *haliotis* shell and human hair (see 81).

On a shaman's arms and wrists, circles of ermine skin or etched horn were often worn like bracelets.

88 (overleaf) A Tlingit shaman's moose-hide apron displaying a painting of fish or sea mammals at the top, a human face at the center, and upside-down confronting animal heads at the bottom. Deer dewclaws are attached to the fringes, and sixty amulets are sewn onto the central area of the apron. Collected by Emmons from a shaman's gravehouse sometime between 1882 and 1887. Length 36" (91.4 cm).

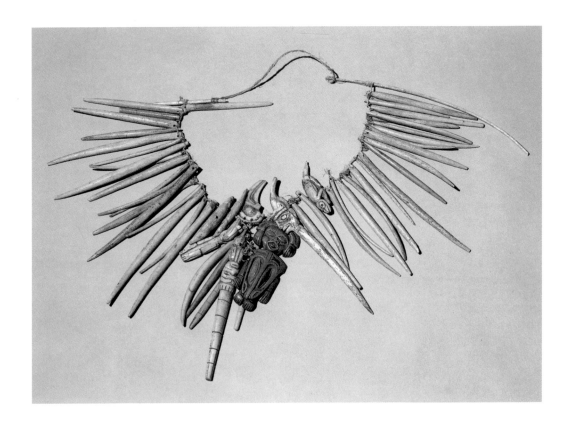

89 The elements making up this necklace could have come from different groups and were perhaps put together at different times. The images on the ten carved amulets include a human wearing a shoulder robe, a man wearing a hat with potlatch rings, as well as various animals and birds. Length of largest amulet 10¼" (26 cm).

A wooden club (91) was frequently carried to assist a practitioner in his fight against hostile spirits. Also, charms were among a shaman's most valuable and highly supernaturally charged possessions. Such amulets (92, 93) were a particularly potent part of every Tlingit shaman's paraphernalia; some were worn as single pendants, others in groups as parts of necklaces (see 89), or sewn onto animal-hide tunics, or onto aprons (see 88). Some charms were left with a patient after a practitioner's performance in order to sustain the shaman's power.[25]

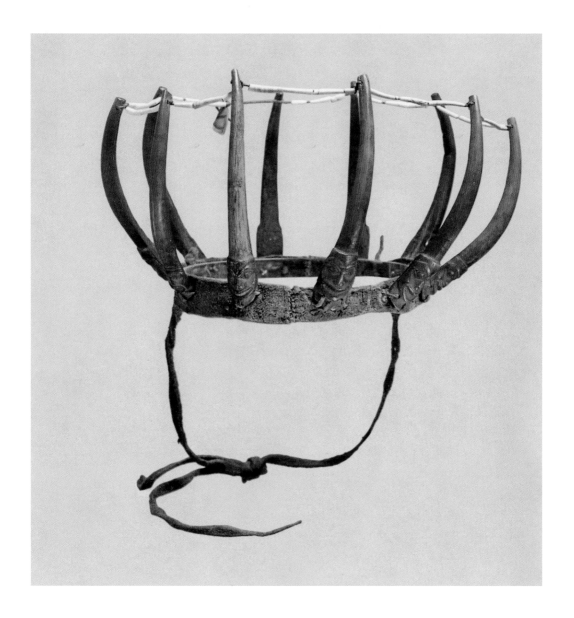

90 A Tlingit shaman's crown of mountain goat horns assembled to represent bear claws. Note that a human head is carved at the base of each horn. Height 6⅞" (17.4 cm).

91 (left) A Tlingit shaman's wooden club, which he used against hostile spirits; the club depicts a frontal face atop a land otter and a raven with a man in its mouth. Length 27" (68. 7 cm).

92 (below) A Tlingit shaman's charm carved from a sperm whale tooth, with abalone shell eyes. This symmetrical arrangement is composed of two opposing figures—perhaps bears—which flank the image of a small central octopus whose beak-like mouth is clearly shown. Length 4" (10 cm).

93 (opposite) A Tlingit shaman's spirit charm used in healing (front and back views). This skeletal figure is carved from ivory and was collected from a Tlingit shaman's kit by George Thornton Emmons in 1894 from the Peril Strait region, which is located 30 miles (48 km) north of Sitka, Alaska. Length 2¼" (5.5 cm).

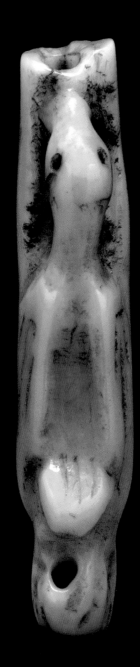
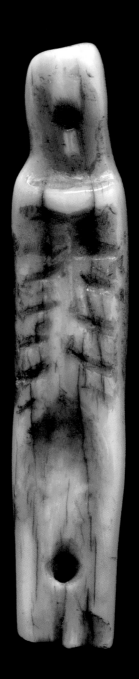

94 A Haida model of a dead shaman's body prepared for placement in his gravehouse. The figures on the flanking posts are guardian spirits who wear the oblong hat sometimes used by practitioners. The raven on the roof represents the crest of the dead shaman. Height 26¼" (66.7 cm).

DEATH AND SUCCESSION

Just as a shaman existed in a world apart during life, so too after death. Among the Tlingit, death was followed by cremation for everyone except a shaman because it was believed that a practitioner's body was impervious to fire. As a result, when a shaman died his body had to be specially prepared for burial: the corpse was carefully arranged and its long, unruly hair was drawn to the top of the head and secured with an ivory or bone pin.[26] Following this preparation, the body was laid out on a board (94), ready to be deposited in a

95 The gravehouse of a Tlingit shaman located on the Chilkat River. Emmons' notes identify this structure as a shaman's grave, but he also published it as a chief's grave. Chiefs, however, were not buried in such structures unless they were shamans. The chief's prestigious Chilkat blanket displayed on the front of this gravehouse suggests that this may well have been the case.

specially constructed gravehouse (95). A storage chest (96) containing the shaman's professional clothing and accoutrements—masks, rattles, skin aprons, crowns, headdresses, clubs, necklaces, charms (98)—was all placed in the gravehouse near the body.[27]

A deceased shaman's ritual paraphernalia sometimes passed on into the hands of a successor. This could occur in one of two ways. When a shaman was dying he sometimes would send for a man he liked, who may even have been his assistant, and tell him that if he

96 (pages 154–155) This outstanding Tlingit shaman's chest has an unusual history. Originally the chest was wrapped in a cedar-bark mat and placed in the hollow of a cedar tree by an unknown shaman, probably in the early 19th century.

97 (opposite) A Tlingit spirit figure created to guard a shaman's gravehouse. This carving depicts a shaman singing; the designs on the costume at the shoulders and over the groin are spirit fish. Rattles were originally held in the spirit figure's hands. Height 61" (155 cm).

98 (above) A display of a shaman's skull and the professional paraphernalia that was removed from a looted gravehouse located near Port Mulgrave, Yakuta.

99 (overleaf) This photograph is captioned, "A water view of two small islands, each crowded with gravehouses." The picture was taken in southeast Alaska, near what may be Shakan Bay.

wanted to become a shaman the dying man would give him all his ritual materials, as well as tell him all his secrets, so that the successor might become just as powerful as his predecessor.[28] Another manner in which a shaman's professional accoutrements came to a new practitioner occurred during the refurbishment of a shamanic gravehouse as a preliminary to a great potlatch honoring the dead. The handling of the remains was done by members of the shaman's opposite moiety, all of whom had fasted; "…among the group were younger clansmen of the deceased, for this was a time when one of them might receive the shamanistic call, it was hoped."[29]

As for the gravehouse itself (see 95), most were square structures built of spruce logs, neatly fitted together and notched at the ends; they rested on four heavy corner posts, and were elevated some 2 ft (60 cm) above the ground. The flooring and roof were of split log shakes, the roof being higher in front and sloping to the rear; the structure was weighted down with cross logs or rocks. These gravehouses, which always faced the water, were sometimes placed on a prominent headland or island (99) where the occupants of passing canoes could offer a sacrifice in the form of a bit of tobacco or food. If children were in the canoe, bird down would be blown over their heads to protect them from the deceased shaman's powerful spirit.[30] The practitioner's body was believed to be guarded always by spirits that had belonged to him in life. In some cases, carved figures representing those spirits were stationed nearby the shaman's gravehouse (97).

WITCHCRAFT

Accompanying shamanism was witchcraft, the darkest aspect of Northwest Coast spiritual life. Unfortunately, witchcraft dominated the Tlingit realm. The anxiety it engendered not only kept people in constant fear of the supernatural but also made them so suspicious of one another that the simplest words or acts could be subject to misunderstanding. Ironically, the whole

100 (opposite) A shaman torturing a witch. This shaman, known as Dr. Pete, was blind in one eye; he wears a crown of mountain sheep horns, a necklace with bone and ivory pendants, an ivory soul catcher, a tunic, and an apron with puffin-beak and deer-dewclaw appendages. In his right hand, he holds an oystercatcher rattle.

101 A free-standing carving of a witch tied up in order to be tortured. Height 8" (20.3 cm).

cult of witchcraft resulted from a shaman's efforts to retain his prestige when his incantations failed to save a patient. In other words, "to save his face," a shaman would denounce someone as a witch who was said to have hated the sick person and hence set out to destroy him. Generally the accused was some poor person, either young or old, with few friends and no following. Sometimes a particularly self-serving shaman even selected a personal enemy to denounce.[31]

So great was the dread of witchcraft, and so deep the shame extending to the family lineage of the one said to be a witch, that the nearest relatives were repeatedly the first to lay hands on the accused and tie the unfortunate creature up to starve to death. Traditionally, the sick person and the accused witch belonged to the same clan or lineage, whereas the shaman belonged to another clan, and often conveniently lived in another village.

Aside from the ordinary sicknesses produced by evil spirits in general, a much more fatal form of disease was directly attributable to witchcraft; this

was the case when a victim's body was "poisoned," as it were, not by an in-
dwelling spirit but rather by the evil practice of some witch skilled in the black
arts. The proposed "murder" was accomplished by secretly procuring—from
the targeted victim—some bodily fluid, a lock of hair, a drop of blood, or a bit
of clothing, which was then made up into a little image intended to represent
the fated person. This "doll" was then placed inside a gravehouse beside the
corpse of a deceased shaman. The well-being of the victim the doll represented was believed to be dependent on this fetish, and as it rotted away its living
counterpart was directly affected, unless the guilty witch was discovered and
denounced by a shaman. The witch was either forced to confess—and hence
undo the evil charm—or put to death.[32]

Once the witch was identified, all friends, as well as the witch's nearest relatives, deserted the accused in terror and shame: indeed, some were the first
to capture, bind, and torture the offender. The witch's arms were tied behind
the back, at the wrists with the palms out, and the hair was wound around a
toggle with a sinew or hide cord. With this cord the head was stretched as far
back as possible toward the wrists and then secured to a low stake driven into
the ground so the body was forced into a kneeling position (100, 101). The
point of the torture was not the death of the witch—after all, if the witch was
dead he or she could not save the victim—but rather to force a confession.
Once this was accomplished, the witch retrieved the effigy, and threw it into
the water, and then "…plunged in himself and rushed ashore, cleansed of
all power of witchcraft forever. He went back to the house of the patient and
wished him good health. If the latter recovered soon, (the victim) might fete
the witch and his family."[33] However, many accused witches were killed early
on, in a rage.

In the opinion of George Thornton Emmons:

"The worst feature of Tlingit life was the shaman and the associated belief
in witchcraft, which made the people suspicious of each other and fearful
of all natural conditions that they could not understand."[34]

PRESERVATION OR THEFT?

Among some present-day Tlingit Indians, Emmons is a controversial figure precisely because they regard his actions as the looting of their ancestors' gravehouses. However, that attitude may not have prevailed at the time that Emmons was active in the area. Frederica de Laguna, the definitive authority on Emmons' research,[35] discusses a problem concerning Emmons that has been noted by several scholars: how was it possible that Emmons repeatedly "was able to list the name of a specific shaman, his clan, the location of his gravehouse, and, more important, the identities of the spirits represented by his masks and other objects?"[36] This is particularly puzzling because the Tlingit are reported to have believed that a person who approached a shaman's grave or handled his things was at risk of serious illness, or death. Nonetheless, "a knowledgeable native must have [assisted] Emmons when he was labeling and cataloging the specimens"[37] that he had removed from each particular gravehouse. The answer may lie in the tenor of the times.

The late 19th century was the period when missionary work was flourishing along the Northwest Coast, and Tlingit communities were vying for missions and schools. Many people, including elders and chiefs, were converting to Christianity. Young people were also ready to turn away from all "heathen" practices, and in so doing escape the heavy burden of emulating their ancestor's potlatches as well as the hardships and dangers associated with a shaman's profession. One way of avoiding such demands from the past was "to have a white man, who apparently could not be injured by the spirits, take away [all of] the dangerous ritual paraphernalia from a gravehouse, just as one might clean up a toxic dump. Any Tlingit assisting Emmons must have sighed with relief when the American packed up his treasures and shipped them off to the United States."[38] And the money paid by the collector also would have been most welcome.

But how could Emmons—always so ready to defend the property rights of the Tlingit—justify collecting items from a shaman's grave? Frederica de Laguna[39] points out an interesting aspect of Emmons' character: he was objective and fair in all of his writing about Tlingit culture except when it came to the cruelties inflicted by shamans on those whom they denounced as witches (see 100, 101). Perhaps the removal of shamanistic paraphernalia, insofar as this could help in suppressing the practice of shamanism, was justi-fied in Emmons' mind as the removal of evil.

Edmund Carpenter, another anthropologist familiar with Tlingit culture, has also pondered de Laguna's query about the Indians assisting Emmons. He notes that some of the world's most prized Tlingit pieces came from Emmons:

> …often directly from shamans' graves. The Tlingits watched Emmons take
> them. This puzzled me until I read that Tlingit masks might be owned by
> successive shamans. Masks weren't abandoned there to rot, but placed
> there to be retrieved by those who, having studied and sacrificed, qualified
> as guardians. Tlingit elders transferred sacred treasures to Emmons,
> whom they trusted. They believed that the power within those objects
> and [the] truths within those myths could survive everything except
> neglect. They had no illusions about their own children. Emmons was
> often their only listener. Emmons saved what he could. He served as a
> surrogate tribal elder when those offices stood empty. He never intended
> to deprive anyone, least of all the Tlingit, of their heritage. He sought only
> to preserve. Without his efforts, what would now survive?[40]

Over the years Emmons' repeated collections of Tlingit grave goods have enhanced the galleries of some of our foremost museums, together with the knowledge contained in his detailed notes on the meaning, function and general cultural significance of the objects he sold to many of our most eminent institutions.[41]

New York's American Museum of Natural History holds what has been called the "largest and finest collection of Northwest Coast Indian art in the world,"[42] as their magnificent Northwest Coast Hall attests. One of the Tlingit's

102 (above) Claude Lévi-Strauss and party being paddled up the Seine in a Tlingit war canoe on October 2, 1989. Monique Lévi-Strauss reports that the canoe departed from the bridge by the Eiffel Tower and traveled to the Hotel de Ville, where the mayor, then Jacques Chirac, received the entire group; the Tlingit then played their drums and sang.

103 (opposite) A model of a crouching canoe prow figurehead painted in the traditional Tlingit colors of red, green, and black. Length 4¼" (10.8 cm).

most esteemed admirers, the French anthropologist Claude Lévi-Strauss (102), has left a memorable accolade to that Hall:

There is in New York a magic place where all the dreams
of childhood hold a rendezvous, where century old tree trunks
sing or speak, where indefinable objects lie in wait for the
visitor with an anxious stare; where animals of superhuman
gentleness press their uplifted little paws, clasped in prayer
for the privilege of constructing for the chosen one the palace
of the beaver, or guiding him into the realm of the seals, or
of teaching him, with a mystic kiss, the language of the frog
and kingfisher.[43]

CONCLUSION

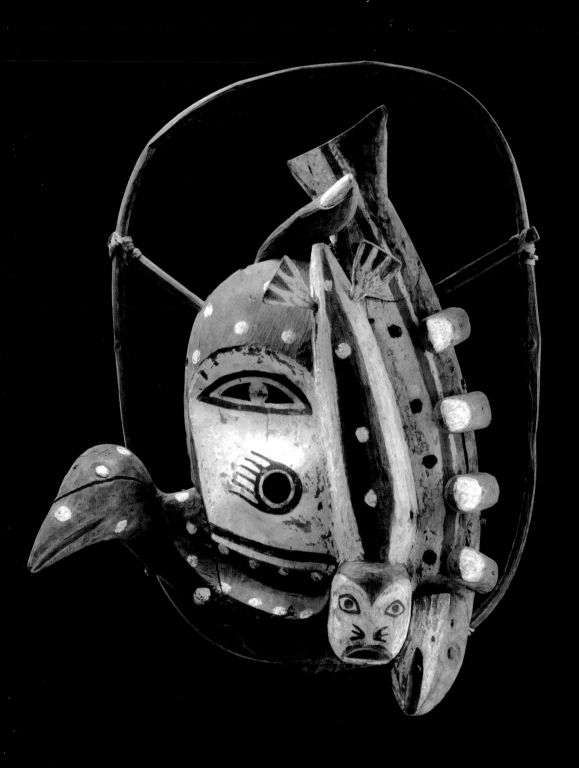

✳

M uch of what we know about the history of the northern peoples can be deduced from their art. The representations of the earliest hunter-gatherers to populate northeast Siberia and America's Far North reflected a belief in a collaborative reciprocity between the vulnerable Arctic hunters and their animal prey. As the anthropologist William W. Fitzhugh explains,[1] such artistic expressions are now known as Hunting Art, which varied according to each group's economic and social condition. The Siberian situation is a case in point.

Some 2,000 years ago the Siberians made two important economic advances: they domesticated reindeer and obtained metallurgy, innovations that never took hold in pre-contact North America. As a result of those changes, the Siberian hunting and herding cultures became more specialized, production-related groups as opposed to subsistence-oriented societies. The professional attire of Siberian shamans reflected the changes in their society: the emphasis of shamanic costumes was on design and ornamentation of the apparel, which no longer reflected a purely animal orientation.

Hunting Art, which is most widely known from the European Upper Paleolithic, is exemplified in the New World by the early artistry of the Alaskan Eskimo. Their lives were completely dependent on their marine prey, hence their art retained its strong animalistic emphasis. For the Eskimo, images of game, weapons, and helping spirits were used to

104 A Yup'ik Eskimo dance mask from Hooper Bay, Alaska. A bentwood hoop, said to signify the outer universe, surrounds a central face partly obscured by a salmon-like fish, a seal with a humanoid face and the head and neck of a sea bird. The entire mask image appears to be held in the palm of a hand. Height 20½" (52 cm).

influence the spirits of the animals; a man's own powers alone were considered weak and ineffectual, and shamanic help was needed. This dependence is reflected in the dramatic, creative drawings and masks that have come down to us from the early Arctic/Alaskan world.

South of the Bering Sea, where communal exploitation of the large, relatively stable fish resources replaced the hunting of marine mammals, different religious views and artistic representations are found. Here the Native art was used primarily to communicate social values through the display of heraldic crests and totemic insignia. Although Tlingit art also functioned as hunting magic on the Northwest Coast, its primary role was in expressing social rank, social organization, and rights of possession.

In all three cultures shamans continued to play critically important roles in society. Even as those roles changed, they were still needed to explain—or at least to control and use—the mysteries and powers that abounded in the realms of spirits, both malign and benevolent. The dress and accoutrements changed with the cultures, but in all cases were dominated by elements that embodied both mystery and power: faces hidden by veils of hanging fringes (Siberia) or by masks (Arctic and Northwest Coast); elaborate costumes emphasizing the rarest and most valuable elements of a culture (metal ornaments in profusion in Siberia, ivory and wooden talismans where metal was not available); and masks of the most exquisite expressiveness and skill of carving. With these material "props," in all cases came musical instruments and dramatic behavior that required specialized training and a lifetime of practice to perfect.

In the final analyses, however, the native art that truly dazzled the mid-20th-century Surrealists were the pieces that came out of the frigid lands of the Arctic and Alaska (104), modern-day reflections of a worldview similar to that found in the Hunting Art of the Upper Paleolithic, an archaic ideology that still miraculously existed in a remote corner of the New World's Far North.

BIBLIOGRAPHY

Anawalt, Patricia R., 2007, *The Worldwide History of Dress*, Thames & Hudson, London

Arutiunov, S. A., 1988, "Even: Reindeer Herders of Eastern Siberia," in Fitzhugh and Crowell, eds, *Crossroads of Continents: Cultures of Siberia and Alaska*, pp. 35–38

Arutiunov, S. A. and William W. Fitzhugh, 1988, "Prehistory of Siberia and the Bering Sea," in Fitzhugh and Crowell, eds, *Crossroads of Continents: Cultures of Siberia and Alaska*, pp. 117–27

Auger, Emily E., 2005, *The Way of Inuit Art: Aesthetics and History in and beyond the Arctic*, McFarland & Co., Inc., Jefferson, NC and London

Bahn, Paul and Jean Vertut, 1997, *Journey Through the Ice Age*, Weidenfeld & Nicolson, London and University of California Press, Berkeley

Bahnson, Anne, 2011, "The Ipiutak Culture: A Mysterious People of the Arctic," in Carpenter, *Upside Down: Arctic Realities*, pp. 162–71

Balter, Michael, 2011, "Tracing the Paths of the First Americans," *Science* Vol. 333: 192

Bolz, Peter and Hans-Ulrich Sanner, 1999, *Native American Art: The Collections of the Ethnological Museum, Berlin*, University of Washington Press, Seattle

Bronshtein, Mikhail and Dneprovsky, Kirill, 2011, "Ancient Eskimo Art of Ekvan: Collection of the State Museum of Oriental Art," in Carpenter, *Upside Down: Arctic Realities*, pp. 120–61

Carpenter, Edmund, 2005, *Two Essays: Chief and Greed*, Persimmon Press, North Andover, MA

Carpenter, Edmund, 2011, *Upside Down: Arctic Realities*. Published on the occasion of the exhibition, "Upside Down: Arctic Realities." The Menil Collection, Houston, distributed by Yale University Press, New Haven

Carpenter, Edmund, 2011a, "Dorset Film," in Carpenter, *Upside Down: Arctic Realities*, pp. 80–85

Carpenter, Edmund, 2011b, "Old Bering Sea," in Carpenter, *Upside Down: Arctic Realities*, pp. 86–117

Carwardine, Mark, 1995/2002, *Whales, Dolphins and Porpoises*, Smithsonian Handbooks, Dorling Kindersley Ltd., London

Davis, Wade, 2009, *The Wayfinders: Why Ancient Wisdom Matters in the Modern World*, Massey lecture series, House of Anansi Press, Toronto, Ontario

Eliade, Mircea, 1964, *Shamanism: Archaic Techniques of Ecstasy*. Translated from the French by Willard R. Trask. Bollingen Series LXXVI. Princeton University Press, Princeton

Ellis, Donald, 2003, *Donald Ellis Gallery Catalog*, Donald Ellis Gallery, Ltd., Toronto

Ellis, Donald, 2007, *Donald Ellis Gallery Catalog*, Donald Ellis Gallery, Ltd., Toronto

Ellis, Donald, 2011, *Donald Ellis Gallery 11*, Donald Ellis Gallery, Ltd., Toronto

Emmons, George Thornton, 1991, *The Tlingit Indians*, University of Washington Press, Seattle, and the American Museum of Natural History, New York

Fienup-Riordan, Ann, 1996, *The Living Tradition of Yupik Masks*, University of Washington Press, Seattle

Fienup-Riordan, Ann, 2011, "The Living Tradition of Yup'ik Masks," in Carpenter, *Upside Down: Arctic Realities*, pp. 198–203

Fitzhugh, William W. and Aron Crowell, eds, 1988, *Crossroads of Continents: Cultures of Siberia and Alaska*, Smithsonian Institution Press, Washington DC

Fitzhugh, William W., Julie Hollowell, and Aron L. Crowell, eds, 2009, *Gifts from the Ancestors: Ancient Ivories of Bering Strait*, Princeton University Art Museum, distributed by Yale University Press, New Haven and London

Frazer, James George, 1936–41, *The Golden Bough: A Study in Magic and Religion*, 3rd edn, 12 vols, Macmillan & Co., London

Gibbons, Ann, 2012, "Genes Suggest Three Groups Peopled the New World," *Science* Vol. 337: 144

Gorbacheva, Valentina and Karina Solovyeva, 2006, *Between Worlds: Shamanism of the Peoples of Siberia*, Khudozhnik i Kniga, Moscow

Gurvich, I. S., 1988, "Ethnic Connections across Bering Strait," in Fitzhugh and Crowell, eds, *Crossroads of Continents: Cultures of Siberia and Alaska*, pp. 17–21

Holm, Bill, 1988, "Art and Culture Change at the Tlingit-Eskimo Border," in Fitzhugh and Crowell, eds, *Crossroads of Continents: Cultures of Siberia and Alaska*, pp. 281–93

Jochelson, Waldemar, 1908, *The Jesup North Pacific Expedition. Memoir of the American Museum of Natural History*, ed. Franz Boas, Vol. VI: *The Koryak*, E. J. Brill, Ltd., Leiden and G. E. Stechert, New York

Jochelson, Waldemar, 1926, *The Jesup North Pacific Expedition. Memoir of the American Museum of Natural History*, ed. Franz Boas, Vol. IX: *The Yukaghir and the Yukaghirized Tungus*, E. J. Brill, Ltd., Leiden and G. E. Stechert, New York

Jochelson, Waldemar, 1933, *Anthropological Papers of The American Museum of Natural History*, Vol. XXXIII, Part II: *The Yakut*, The American Museum of Natural History, New York

Jonaitis, Aldona, 1988, *From the Land of the Totem Poles: The Northwest Coast Indian Art Collection at the American Museum of Natural History*, University of Washington Press, Seattle, and the American Museum of Natural History, New York

Jones, Suzi, ed., 2003, *Eskimo Drawings*, Anchorage Museum of History and Art in association with Anchorage Museum Association

Josephy, Alvin M. Jr., 1994, *500 Nations: An Illustrated History of North American Indians*, Alfred A. Knopf, New York

Kasten, Erich, 2009, *Schamanen Sibiriens: Magier, Mittler, Heiler*, Linden-Museum, Stuttgart

Kehoe, Alice Beck, 2000, *Shamans and Religion: An Anthropological Exploration in Critical Thinking*, Waveland Press, Inc., Prospect Heights, Illinois

Laguna, Frederica de, 1988, "Tlingit: People of the Wolf and Raven," in Fitzhugh and Crowell, eds, *Crossroads of Continents: Cultures of Siberia and Alaska,* pp. 58–63

Lévi-Strauss, Claude, 1943, "The Art of the Northwest Coast at the American Museum of Natural History," in *Gazette des Beaux-Arts* 24: 175–82

Mason, Owen K., 2009, "Art, Power and Cosmos in Bering Strait Prehistory," in Fitzhugh, Hollowell, and Crowell, eds, *Gifts from the Ancestors: Ancient Ivories of Bering Strait*, pp. 112–25

McGhee, Robert and Patricia Sutherland, 2011, "The Art of the Dorset People," in Carpenter, *Upside Down: Arctic Realities*, The Menil Collection, Houston, pp. 46–79

Prins, Harald E. L. and Bunny McBride, 2011, "Upside Down: Arctic Realities and Indigenous Art," Review Essay in *American Anthropologist* Vol. 114(1): 2–18

Ray, Dorothy Jean, 2003, "Happy Jack and Guy Kakarook: Their Art and Their Heritage," in Jones, ed., *Eskimo Drawings*, pp. 19–35

Rousselot, Jean-Loup, William W. Fitzhugh, and Aron Crowell, 1988, "Maritime Economies of the North Pacific Rim," in Fitzhugh and Crowell, eds, *Crossroads of Continents: Cultures of Siberia and Alaska*, pp. 151–72

Sonne, Birgitte, 1988, *Agayut: Nunivak Eskimo Masks and Drawings from the Fifth Thule Expedition 1921–24, Collected by Knud Rasmussen*, Report of the Fifth Thule Expedition, Vol. X, Part 4, Gyldendal, Denmark

Vitebsky, Piers, 2001, *Shamanism*, University of Oklahoma Press, Norman

Wardwell, Allen, 2009, *Tangible Visions: Northwest Coast Indian Shamanism and its Art*, Monacelli Press, with the Corvus Press, New York

NOTES

Introduction : 7–17

1. Eliade 1964: 145.
2. For an explanation of the use of the term "Eskimo," please see note 3 in Part II (p. 179).
3. Wardwell 2009: 10, 12.
4. Auger 2005: 66.
5. Kehoe: 2000.
6. Considering how conservative and unchanging worldwide shamanic practices have proven to be, such criticism of Eliade's use of modern ethnographic accounts would seem unfair.
7. Davis, 2009: 28 *The Wayfinders*.
8. Bahn and Vertut, 1997: 207–8.
9. The New Age movement is a non-religious, spiritual trend, which developed in the latter half of the 20th century and which emphasizes that the mind, body, and spirit are interrelated.
10. Bahn and Vertut 1997: 211.
11. Vitebsky 2001: 6–7, 46. The shamanic specialist, Piers Vitebsky, when speaking of native South and Central American cultures, points out that the shaman is a dominant figure in many of these societies. Also, despite the great distance from the Bering Strait, South American shamanism bears striking similarities to forms of shamanism in Siberia, the source of Native Americans' migrations. The similarities to Siberia are perhaps the strongest evidence for the basic durability of shamanic ideas over the widest range of environments, social structures, and historical periods.
12. Fitzhugh and Crowell 1988: 12.
13. Fitzhugh and Crowell 1988: 9.

I
Siberia : 19–69

1. See Balter 2011: 192 and Gibbons 2012: 144 for further information on the peopling of the Far North.
2. Fitzhugh and Crowell 1988: 13.
3. Arutiunov 1988: 36–37.
4. Vitebsky 2001: 84.
5. Vitebsky 2001: 83.

6. Gorbacheva and Solovyeva 2006: 111.

7. Gorbacheva and Solovyeva 2006: 111.

8. The Siberian shamans' single-headed drum was seldom used for amusement or to sound an alarm; the drum primarily served as an instrument for shamanic performances (Jochelson 1933: 120).

9. Gorbacheva and Solovyeva 2006: 110, 111, 128, 138, 146, 172.

10. Jochelson 1908: 47. The Siberian shamans' guarding spirits are remarkably like those of the North American Indians.

11. Gorbacheva and Solovyeva 2006: 18.

12. Gorbacheva and Solovyeva 2006: 21. The St. Petersburg's Russian Museum of Ethnography is not to be confused with the Peter the Great Museum of Anthropology and Ethnography (Kuntskamera) founded by Peter the Great in 1714, and also located in St. Petersburg.

13. Gorbacheva and Solovyeva 2006: 18–19.

14. Jochelson early on had also worked with the Yakut in 1884 to 1894; subsequently he made collections among that same group from 1900 to 1902 for the Jesup North Pacific Expedition (Jochelson 1933: 37).

15. Jochelson 1908: 49.

16. Jochelson 1908: 51.

17. Gorbacheva and Solovyeva 2006: 270.

18. Gorbacheva and Solovyeva 2006: 248.

19. Gorbacheva and Solovyeva 2006: 248.

20. Gorbacheva and Solovyeva 2006: 248.

21. Gorbacheva and Solovyeva 2006: 248.

22. Kasten 2009: 150.

23. Jochelson 1908: 48.

24. Gorbacheva and Solovyeva 2006: 124.

25. The Nemets, whose main activity was reindeer herding, have a revealing saying, "Without reindeer the tundra has none of life's comforts" (Gorbacheva and Solovyeva 2006: 74). It would appear that Comfort, like Beauty, is in the eye of the beholder.

26. In the Caucasus Mountains, the Iron Age began ca. 1200 BC (Elizabeth Barber: personal communication).

27. Gorbacheva and Solovyeva 2006: 163.

28. Arutiunov and Fitzhugh 1988: 120.

29. Arutiunov and Fitzhugh 1988: 120.

II
The Arctic and Alaska: Eskimo : 71–117

1.   See note 12 below.

2.   The Eskimo believed that if they showed attention and respect to the sea mammals and their spirits, the animals would reciprocate with the willing gifts of their flesh and lives.

3.   The following quote comes from "Notes on the Word Eskimo" (Carpenter 2011: 9).

"The modern aboriginal people of the Arctic regions commonly called Eskimo are not a uniform culture or race. They are a complex chain of heritages spreading across vast regions. In general, however, they are divided into four main branches: the *Yup'ik* of Southern Alaska, the Siberian *Yup'ik* of Siberia and St. Lawrence Island, the *Inupiat* of Northern Alaska, and the *Inuit* of Canada and Greenland. They share a common ancestry and linguistic origins from the ancient Thule culture. There is a great deal of linguistic continuity among the Inuit across all regions, whereas the Yup'ik speak four distinct languages depending upon the region. The Chukchi people, as the Yup'ik living in Siberia are known, have additional language variants and dialects. Understandably, there are widely differing attitudes within these native Arctic communities as to the collective name Eskimo.

There is no consensus on an acceptable term to define all aboriginal Arctic peoples. To the Inuit, 'Eskimo' is perceived as derogatory, and the word is no longer in common use in Canada or Greenland. To the Yup'ik, however, there is no such association, and to some the term 'Eskimo' is preferred, since it includes both the Inuit and Yup'ik peoples, and for them to use the term 'Inuit' to define themselves would be incorrect. As such, 'Eskimo' remains in common use in the United States and Russia."

4.   Prins and McBride 2011: 3.

5.   For an expanded discussion of the peopling of the New World, see Balter 2011: 195.

6.   McGhee and Sutherland 2011: 46–47.

7.   McGhee and Sutherland 2011: 48.

8.   McGhee and Sutherland 2011: 48.

9.   Carpenter 2011: 89.

10. Bronshtein and Dneprovsky, 2011: 127.

11. Bahnson, 2011: 168–69.

12. Fitzhugh and Crowell 2009: 206.

13. Fitzhugh and Crowell 2009: 206.

14. "The Gray Whale is known for the 12,400 mile (20,000 km) round trip between its southern breeding grounds in Baja, California, Mexico, and its northern feeding grounds in the Bering, Chukchi, and Beaufort Seas. This is one of the longest known migrations of any known mammal" (Carwardine 2002: 50).

15. Rousselot, Fitzhugh and Crowell 1988: 163, 166, 168.
16. Ray 2003: 19.
17. Gurvich 1988: 21.
18. Account of the naked lady: "In the spring of 1948 I was hunting after ice breakup. I had six men hunting with me in my omiak. Somehow that day hardly any seals or oogruk and we caught few seals and headed home. We stopped on a big ice pack thinking we might see oogruk on the ice and then just when we said something, the weather started to get a little foggy. Ran Nineguelook got his binoculars and spoke softly that there was a woman sitting on the ice.

    He told me to come and see for myself if I wanted to see it, but, as he was my first cousin, I didn't because he would just be fooling me. Other men saw it and said it was a human being, so I finally looked through the binoculars and saw a woman with long hair and a red skin tied around her head, but she was sitting sideways. But it was a woman. She would look a little bit our way but not directly toward us.

    Other people who saw them with fish fins from the waist down but the one we saw had legs like us. There have been lots of other stories about that they have seen at Wales, at Cape Espenberg, and Teller, Buckland, and other places. Many people, tourists, say how can you say you saw a woman with no clothes on—it cannot be. But it was true in June of 1948.

    My crew's names were Ray Nineguelook Arthur Tocktoo, Vincent Lockton, Carson Tingook, Jackie Mingoona, and a young boy (dictated to Bessie Moses)" (Jones 2003: 112).
19. Sonne 1988: 9.
20. Sonne 1988: 40
21. Sonne 1988: 40.
22. Fitzhugh and Crowell 1988: 305.
23. Fienup-Riordan 2011: 198.
24. The Agayuyaraq Festival is also sometimes referred to as *Kelek*.
25. See Fienup-Riordan 1996 for an impressive array of extant Yup'ik masks.
26. Fienup-Riordan 1996: 77–84.
27. John McIntyre's mask, which features a stylized sailing ship, reflects a legend passed on to him by his ninety-two-year-old grandmother, Minnie Carter: Long ago a Yup'ik shaman named Issiisaiyuk—who lived at the mouth of the Kuskokwim River—predicted the coming of the white man in the initial form of an uncanny sailing ship filled with strange people. The shaman warned the villagers not to trade with these pale-skinned strangers as they were really spirits up to no good. The villagers ignored this advice only to find that when the ship sailed away their trade goods faded into nothing.

    The following summer of 1778, an actual sailing ship under the command of Captain Cook docked outside the same village. Cook wrote in his ship's log that the local Natives

acted in a strange manner, yelling and throwing furs and other things onboard in order
to trade for the white man's goods. McIntyre contends that Cook's notation represents
written history corroborating his people's oral tradition.

28. Fienup-Riordan 1996: 11.

29. Ellis 2011: 24.

30. Ellis 2011: 24.

31. Claude Lévi-Strauss is quoted as saying, "I was reluctant to become the owner of
such fragile masterpieces and to feel responsible for their safe keeping to future
generations. I even doubted that those masks belonged to the solid world of objects.
I rather saw them as fleeting and almost immaterial embodiments of words, visions,
and beliefs, eluding durable possession" (Claude Lévi-Strauss: September 18, 1994
[Fienup-Riordan 1996: 215]).

Fienup-Riordan (1996: 261) notes that Lévi-Strauss' "heady" initial introduction to
North American art and mythology deflected him from his work in the Amazon and
marked the beginning of his development of Structural Anthropology. "He saw in the
masks evidence of the 'deep structures' of the human mind, structures he spent the
rest of his life elaborating." (*ibid.*)

32. Ellis 2011: 24, 26.

33. Martin Sauer, 1802, *An account of a geographical and astronomical expedition to the
northern parts of Russia, for ascertaining the degrees of latitude and longitude of the mouth
of the river Kovima; of the whole coast of the Tshutski, to East Cape: and of the islands in the
eastern ocean, stretching to the American coast. Performed...by Commodore Joseph Billings,
in the years 1785–1794. The whole narrated from the original papers, by Martin Sauer*
(T. Cadell, London). Quoted by Fitzhugh and Crowell 1988: 12.

III
The Northwest Coast : 119–167

1. Holm 1988: 156–57.

2. Some male Tlingits are said to have had deformed legs as the result of spending so
much time crouched down while paddling a canoe (Emmons 1991: 15).

3. Anawalt 2007: 346–47.

4. Fitzhugh and Crowell 1988: 16.

5. Holm 1988: 288.

6. I am indebted to Dr. Kathleen Whitaker for this insight into the exchange of Tlingit
relationship information.

7. De Laguna 1988: 60.

8. De Laguna 1988: 60.

9. Ellis 2003: 42.

10. Emmons 1991: 226. See Emmons 1991: 224 for the origin of the Chilkat blanket among the Tsimshian.

11. Wardwell 2009: 9–10.

12. Wardwell 2009: 16–18.

13. The Tlingit uneasiness about menstrual fluids persists. During the Annual Meeting of the International Society of Shamanic Research—May 28 to June 1, 2009, Anchorage, Alaska—the Tlingit elder Bob Sam displayed a revered Tlingit shaman's mask (see illustration 13). The audience was invited to step forward to admire the mask at closer range, except for any women in their menses.

14. Jonaitis 1988: 93.

15. Wardwell 2009: 6.

16. Emmons 1991: 385.

17. There were several interesting aspects to George Emmons' character. Despite having an American wife, Kittee Baker, and two children, with whom he lived in Sitka, Emmons also had a Tlingit family. According to Bob Sam, an elder of the Tlingit Dog Salmon Clan, Emmons was "involved with" the daughter (?) of Chief Kowee, who was an important shaman of the Eagle Moiety, Kaawa.ee of the Dog Salmon House, Léemaidi clan, Tlingit tribe.

    Bob Sam stumbled on this information when he visited the National Museum of the American Indian in Washington and the American Museum of Natural History in New York to negotiate the repatriation of all of the contents from the gravehouse of the shaman Chief Kowee, which included the memorable mask shown in illustration 13. In the course of going through records found in both museums, Bob Sam was startled to find that he, himself, was a direct descendant—in fact, a great-grandson—of George Emmons, a man Sam had always held in low regard. (Research alert: unsettling facts may lie in wait.)

    The above information was divulged by Bob Sam at the Annual Meeting of the International Society for Shamanic Research held in Anchorage, Alaska, May 28–June 1, 2009, in the session, "Forum on Repatriation and Shamanism." Sam's presentation was entitled, "A Tlingit Shaman's Mask." Dr. Kathleen Whitaker, the author's Research Associate, was in the audience and took detailed notes.

18. Emmons 1991: xvii. Emmons wrote, "…I have made a study of their history [the Chilkat and Chilkoot people] and I have lived among them on the most intimate terms, until they have given me one of their family names and look upon me as one of themselves…" Frederica de Laguna points out that Emmons never revealed the actual name given him, which group gave it to him, or to what clan that name belonged.

19. Wardwell 2009: 10.

20. Emmons 1991: 377.

21. Emmons 1991: 377.
22. Emmons 1991: 376.
23. Jonaitis 1988: 100.
24. When the author and Dr. Kathleen Whitaker visited the archive of the Museum of the North, located in Fairbanks, Alaska, their request to examine a Tlingit shaman's necklace proved a disconcerting experience: they were told that no woman's hand was allowed to touch the necklace, at the request of Tlingit tribal leaders.
25. Wardwell 2009: 165; Emmons 1991: 385.
26. Emmons 1991: 391–97.
27. Emmons 1991: 394–95.
28. Emmons 1991: 397.
29. Emmons 1991: 280–81.
30. Emmons 1991: 394.
31. Emmons 1991: 398.
32. Emmons 1991: 399–403.
33. Emmons 1991: 403.
34. Emmons 1991: 370.
35. Frederica de Laguna is *the* definitive authority on Emmons' research, as the result of being the scholar who finally completed his long-delayed book. When Emmons died in 1945, his monograph on the Tlingit Indians—started around 1888—remained unfinished. However, there were several drafts of his manuscript in the American Museum of Natural History and also in the British Columbia Archives in Victoria. It was the anthropologist Frederica de Laguna—herself very familiar with the Tlingit world, because she had carried out years of fieldwork there—who finished Emmons' work, over one hundred years later, augmented with her own knowledgeable additions (Emmons 1991: xi).
36. Emmons 1991: xii.
37. Emmons 1991: xix.
38. Emmons 1991: xviii.
39. Emmons 1991: xviii.
40. Carpenter 2005: 63.
41. Jonaitis 1988: 87.
42. Jonaitis 1988: 12.
43. Claude Lévi-Strauss' accolade to the American Museum of Natural History's Northwest Coast Hall (1943: 175).

Conclusion : 169–172

1. Fitzhugh and Crowell 1988: 295.

ACKNOWLEDGMENTS

My sincere thanks to all of the scholars and institutions listed below for their indispensable assistance with the research reflected in this book.

Dr. Kathleen Whitaker, for our adventurous and memorable field seasons together.

Two UCLA colleagues for their consistent support of this book:
Dr. Alan Grinnell, gifted reader and editor, and Barbara Sloan,
commander of an impressive range of skills.

Dr. Gaby Frank, Frankfurt, Germany, who provided contact information
to European curators.

Julie Jones, Curator Emerita, Department of the Arts of Africa, Oceania and the Americas,
The Metropolitan Museum of Art, New York, for her consistent support.

SIBERIA – 2009

Many thanks to the scholars and institutions that provided access to and
information on their Siberian shaman collections and materials:

Sonia Schiele, curator of the exhibition *Schamanen Sibiriens*,
Linden Museum, Stuttgart, Germany.

Timothy D. Edwards, Editor, *New German Review,* and Agnes Stauber,
Fowler Museum at UCLA, translators of the catalog *Schamanen Sibiriens.*

Dr. Peter Bolz, Staatliche Ethnologisches Museum, Dahlem, Berlin.
Steffan Brunius, Dr. Anders Bjorklund, Anne Murray and Dr. Hakan Wahlquist,
Folken Museet Ethnografiska, Stockholm, Sweden.

Dr. Laila Williamson and Dr. Kristin Olson, American Museum of Natural History,
New York.

ALASKA 2009–2010

Alaska Native Heritage Center.

Alaska Heritage Museum at Wells Fargo.

Alaska Museum of Natural History.

Anchorage Museum at Rasmussen Center.

Sorrell Goodwin, Dr. Steve Henrikson, and Dr. Bob Banghart, Alaska State Museum,
Juneau, Alaska.

James Simard (EED), Alaska State Library and Historical Collections, Juneau, Alaska.

Tripp's Mt. Juneau Trading Post, Juneau, Alaska.

Ryan Lee Oyagak, Inupiat Cultural Center, Barrow, Alaska.

John McIntyre, Mary Woods, and Darlene Orr, Yupiit Piciryarait Cultural Center, Bethel, Alaska.

Dr. Molly Lee, Curator Emerita, Museum of the North, University of Alaska, Fairbanks.

The Sheldon Jackson Museum, Haines, Alaska.

The Northern Arctic Cultural Museum, Kotzebue, Alaska.

George Foot, and Richard Benneville, Nome, Alaska.

Laura Samuelson, The Carrie Mcclain Museum, Nome, Alaska.

Norbert Kakaryk and his sister Sarah, Teller, Alaska.

Rosemary Carlton, The Sheldon Jackson Museum, Sitka, Alaska.

Museum of Skagway, Skagway, Alaska.

The Burke Museum, Seattle, Washington.

Doris, Roland and Julian Flak, Gallerie Flak, Paris, France.

NORTHWEST COAST

Monique Lévi-Strauss, Paris, France.

Dr. Carl Johan Gurt, Folken-Museet Ethnografiska, Stockholm, Sweden.

Dr. Martha Black and Brian Seymour, The Royal British Columbia Museum, Victoria, British Columbia.

The Museum of Anthropology, Vancouver, British Columbia.

Rosemary Carlton, The Sheldon Jackson Museum, Sitka, Alaska.

Museum of Skagway, Skagway, Alaska.

The Burke Museum, Seattle, Washington.

My particular thanks to Donald Ellis, Donald Ellis Gallery, New York, a valued scholar of Native American art, as well as to Carolyn Jones and Nick Jakins and the whole team at Thames & Hudson, for all of their excellent work. And, once again, with tremendous gratitude to Jamie Camplin, Managing Director, Thames & Hudson.

PICTURE CREDITS

Maps on pp. 14–15, 16, 24–25, 74–75 and 127 by Lisa Ifsits. Maps 1, 3, 4 and 5 based on original map artwork by Dr. John M. D. Pohl. Map 2 based on Piers Vitebsky, *Shamanism* (University of Oklahoma Press, Norman, 2001) p. 44.
Drawings on pp. 7, 19, 71, 92, and 119 by Nick Jakins.

Frontispiece: Donald Ellis Gallery, New York.
1   Russian Museum of Ethnography, St. Petersburg. Nos. 163-1a,b; 1572-6; 1757-3; 4871-250; 5589-40/1,2. Photo Alexei Kolmykov, Sergey Polyvyanny
2   Alaska State Library, Thwaites Collection, "Eskimo Medicine Man Exorcising Evil Spirits from a Sick Boy." Neg. PCA-18-497
3   American Museum of Natural History, New York, #335775
4   American Museum of Natural History, New York
5   Russian Museum of Ethnography, St. Petersburg. No. 4447-1. Photo Alexei Kolmykov, Sergey Polyvyanny.
6   Russian Museum of Ethnography, St. Petersburg. No. 3039-13. Photo Alexei Kolmykov, Sergey Polyvyanny
7   US Department of Indian Affairs. William Noah
8   American Museum of Natural History, New York, Image #70/8336, Field 153
9   American Museum of Natural History, New York, Image #70/5620B, Field 93
10 Russian Museum of Ethnography, St. Petersburg. No. 147-5/18. Photo Alexei Kolmykov, Sergey Polyvyanny
11 Russian Museum of Ethnography, St. Petersburg. No. 650-72. Photo Alexei Kolmykov, Sergey Polyvyanny
12 Russian Museum of Ethnography, St. Petersburg. No.1767-6. Photo Alexei Kolmykov, Sergey Polyvyanny
13 Russian Museum of Ethnography, St. Petersburg. Nos. 2105-1; 6779–85/1,2. Photo Alexei Kolmykov, Sergey Polyvyanny
14 American Museum of Natural History, New York, Negative #337626
15 American Museum of Natural History, New York, Negative #1610
16 American Museum of Natural History, New York, Negative #70/5163
17 American Museum of Natural History, New York, Negative #70/5165
18 American Museum of Natural History, New York, Negative #70/5166
19 American Museum of Natural History, New York, Negative #70/5166
20 American Museum of Natural History, New York, Negative #70/5164A,B
21 American Museum of Natural History, New York, Negative #70/5167A,B
22 Russian Museum of Ethnology, St. Petersburg. No. 1374-1. Photos Alexei Kolmykov, Sergey Polyvyanny
23 Russian Museum of Ethnology, St. Petersburg. No. 1374-1. Photos Alexei Kolmykov, Sergey Polyvyanny
24 Russian Museum of Ethnology, St. Petersburg. No. 1374-1. Photos Alexei Kolmykov, Sergey Polyvyanny
25 Russian Museum of Ethnology, St. Petersburg, No. 273-1,2,6,8. Photos Alexei Kolmykov, Sergey Polyvyanny
26 Russian Museum of Ethnology, St. Petersburg, No. 273-1,2,6,8. Photos Alexei Kolmykov, Sergey Polyvyanny
27 American Museum of Natural History, New York, Negative #70/3892

28 American Museum of Natural History, New York, Negative #703386
29 American Museum of Natural History, New York, Negative #4164
30 Russian Museum of Ethnology, St. Petersburg. No. 4216-489,491,496. Photos Alexei Kolmykov, Sergey Polyvyanny
31 Russian Museum of Ethnology, St. Petersburg. No. 4216-489,491,496. Photos Alexei Kolmykov, Sergey Polyvyanny
32 Russian Museum of Ethnology, St. Petersburg. Nos. 1712-245a,b,c,d. Photo Alexei Kolmykov, Sergey Polyvyanny
33 Russian Museum of Ethnology, St. Petersburg. No. 1923-2/1-6. Photo Alexei Kolmykov, Sergey Polyvyanny
34 Russian Museum of Ethnology, St. Petersburg, No. 8761-10128. Photo Alexei Kolmykov, Sergey Polyvyanny
35 Russian Museum of Ethnology, St. Petersburg, No. 1871-44. Photo Alexei Kolmykov, Sergey Polyvyanny
36 Russian Academy of Sciences, Siberian Branch, Kn.63-48090
38 Private collection
39 Canadian Museum of Civilization, Quebec, PfFm-1:1728, IMG2008-0215-0015-Dm
40 Canadian Museum of Civilization, Quebec, PeHb-1:1, IMG2008-0215-0012-Dm
41 Canadian Museum of Civilization, Quebec, NhHd-1:2655, IMG2008-0215-0011-Dm
42 Canadian Museum of Civilization, Quebec, KbFk-7:308, IMG2008-0215-0008-Dm
43 The State Museum of Oriental Art, Moscow.
44 National Museum, Copenhagen, Accession no. P4790
45 National Museum of Copenhagen, Accession nos. P4690, P8197, P4689, P4410-1, P4109, P3973
46 Private collection. Photo Don Cole
47 Private collection. Photo Don Cole
48 Dorling Kindersley, Ltd., London, image ID:20134747
49 Private collection. Photo Don Cole
50 Reprinted from Thomas Pennant, *Arctic Zoology* (Henry Hughes, London, 1784) pl. 6, 144
51 Alaska State Library, James Wickersham Papers, MS107-73-6-27. Photo Cam Byrnes
52 Unnamed artist; from Birgitte Sonne, *Agayut: Nunivak Eskimo Masks and Drawings from the Fifth Thule Expedition 1921–24, Collected by Knud Rasmussen*, Report of the Fifth Thule Expedition, Vol. X, Part 4 (Gyldendal, Denmark, 1988), p. 11
53 Anchorage Museum of History and Art, gift of the Anchorage Museum Foundation, 2002, 002, 008. Photo Chris Arend
54 Alaska State Museum, Juneau, V-A-544 (watercolor by K. Moses)
55 Ethnological Museum, Berlin, Jacobsen Collection, 1883, Inv. Nr.-IV A 5147
56 Museum für Volkerkund, Berlin, IVA7195
57 Sheldon Jackson Museum, Sitka, IIG.11. Photo Barry McWayne
58 Donald Ellis Collection
59 University of Alaska Museum, Fairbanks, UA314-4351
60 Sheldon Jackson Museum, Sitka, IIB8
61 Alaska State Museum, Juneau, 202-E
62 Sheldon Jackson Museum, Sitka, II.3-171. Photo Barry McWayne
63 Photo Bill Roth, 1994
64 Donald Ellis Collection
65 National Museum of the American Indian, Smithsonian Institution, #9/3430
66 Sheldon Jackson Museum, Sitka, IIB45, IIB46
67 Donald Ellis Collection
68 Sheldon Jackson Museum, Sitka, IIF.43. Photo Nadia Jackinsky
69 Alaska State Library, Louis Choris Photograph Collection

—

70   Rock Foundation, New York, A8169a
71   American Museum of Natural History, New York, #328740 (Merrill photograph, 1904)
72   University of Pennsylvania, University Museum, Philadelphia, 14771
73   American Museum of Natural History, New York #24421 (Maynard photograph, 1879)
74   British Columbia Provincial Archives, Victoria. Photo G. T. Emmons
75   Peter the Great Museum of Anthropology and Ethnography, St. Petersburg, No.2520-2
76   Private collection
77   Edward and Cheri Silver Collection
78   National Museum of the American Indian, Smithsonian Institution, #9/7935
79   Fowler Museum at UCLA, Los Angeles, FMX65.10071. Photo Don Cole
80   American Museum of Natural History, New York.
81   American Museum of Natural History, New York, #41618
82   National Museum of the American Indian, Smithsonian Institution, #39/7989
83   American Museum of Natural History, New York, #E3501
84   American Museum of Natural History, New York, #E2684
85   American Museum of Natural History, New York (Photo Winter and Pond, ca. 1894)
86   American Museum of Natural History, New York, #19/812
87   National Museum of the American Indian, Smithsonian Institution #8/1650
88   American Museum of Natural History, New York, #19/1040
89   Haida necklace, Canadian Museum of Civilization, Quebec, VII-B-56, D2002-002893
90   American Museum of Natural History, New York, #19/1010
91   American Museum of Natural History, New York, #19/1161
92   Donald Ellis Collection
93   American Museum of Natural History, New York, #E/678
94   American Museum of Natural History, New York, #16/739
95   American Museum of Natural History, New York #335778
96   Private collection
97   American Museum of Natural History, New York, #E1915
98   Princeton University Art Museum. Photo Donald Baird
99   Alaska State Library, Clarence L. Andrews Photograph Collection, #P45-668
100 Alaska State Library, Edward DeGroff Photograph Collection, #P91-28
101 Alaska State Museum, Juneau, #II-B-1955, Accession #89-12-84
102 Photo Monique Lévi-Strauss
103 Private collection
104 Donald Ellis Collection

INDEX